THIS
A Book for

THIS IS LIFE

A Book for the Busy

by

A Religious of C.S.M.V.

SCM PRESS LTD
56 BLOOMSBURY STREET
LONDON

FIRST PUBLISHED 1960
© SCM PRESS LTD 1960
PRINTED IN GREAT BRITAIN BY
BILLING AND SONS LTD
GUILDFORD AND LONDON

CONTENTS

CONTENTS

I

INTRODUCTION

'WHAT A LIFE!'
'Such is life!'
'While there's life, there's hope.'
'I am come that they might have life, and have it abundantly.'[1]
'This is life eternal, that they might know thee . . . and Jesus Christ . . .'[2]

Human language is at its best inadequate for the expression of human thought, and men have always more ideas than words. In consequence, one word has often to do duty for several conceptions; the word 'life' is a case in point. Of the five quotations at the head of this chapter, three are from common speech, and two from the sayings of our Lord Jesus Christ; and between them they include three senses of the one word 'life'. In 'While there's life, there's hope,' it means biological life, the opposite of biological death, and the meaning is that, as long as a spark of that bodily life remains, as long, that is, as the heart continues to tick over, there is still hope of the sick man's recovery. In 'What a life!' and 'Such is life!' 'life' means the circumstances under

[1] John 10.10.   [2] John 17.3.

7

which the speaker lives, and the tone of voice in which the words are usually said implies that these leave much to be desired, though of course a change of tone could give them a very different and indeed the opposite force. A busy mother might say 'What a life!' in the ordinary sense when the milk boils over and the doorbell rings and the baby is teething and the ex-baby has shut its finger in the door and she herself is fighting influenza on her feet, all more or less at once. Most busy people feel like saying it sometimes, when the demands made on their time and energy outrun the supply. It expresses a sense of frustration, of not having a chance. But when you come to look at it, what is it that is hindered by the press of circumstance, that—so it seems—is being choked in you, and has not room to grow? It is your *life*, in yet another sense. Your bodily life is included, but is the least important part of it. It is your whole self that is thus imperilled and straitened; you feel you have not space or leisure to become yourself.

But wait a minute. You, as a Christian, can truly realize yourself only in so far as you are joined to God in Christ. Without him, as he said himself, you can do nothing; as the branches of a vine can bear fruit only as long as they continue to be part of it, and share its life, exactly so is it with you and me and our relationship to him.[1] If we have any life at all, in the true sense, it is his life in us; as St Paul says, it is 'not I, but Christ that liveth in me'.[2] This fact is absolutely basic. We are very far from grasping it in all its fullness—that is why

[1] John 15.5.   [2] Gal. 2.20.

we are so largely ineffective and have so little joy; yet in a dim sort of way we do recognize its truth. We are all aware of something in us that our circumstances seem to choke, as weeds choke growing corn, something that struggles, something that feels frustrated. When we look into it, we see that something as the very life of Christ in us, the life that he took flesh that we might have, and have abundantly, the life that consists in knowing his Father and himself. If that is quenched, instinctively we feel we shall be nothing. Thus the matter is quite literally one of life and death, and it is our instinct of self-preservation, operating on the highest plane, that makes us react as we do, and feel that we must fight, as it were for breath. But here we are, with 'life' like that, and inescapable. So what?

That is the problem to which we have to try to find an answer in this book. To this end we shall do two things. First we shall consider what the Bible teaches in regard to life, and what 'life' really means. We shall need three chapters for that, two for the Old Testament and one for the New. They will be meaty ones too, and that is not the last that you will hear about the Bible either. You have been warned; but please be patient. It may be you have so far only scratched the surface of the most fruitful field of Holy Scripture and, having reaped small harvest, are inclined to think there is not much more to be got from it. In fact, the field is rich beyond all thought, and inexhaustible, and one of our main objects in this book is to send you back to plough it a bit deeper, for your own enormous profit and delight.

9

We give full references; we humbly hope that you will look them up. This by the way. To go back to our scheme, when we have got the Bible teaching about life, we shall go on, in the ensuing chapters, to think how it applies in all the circumstances, departments and activities of our own life today. This ought to leave us saying 'What a life!' in a quite different way.

2

'LIFE' IN THE OLD TESTAMENT: I

OUR LORD, as we have noted, said, 'I am come that they might have life, and have it abundantly.' He also said, 'I came not to destroy, but to fulfil.'[1]

At Cana, at the beginning of his ministry, he told the servants, when the wine ran short, to fill the waterpots with water, and they filled them up to the brim. Then they filled their pitchers from the pots, and what they took in them was wine.[2]

All our Lord's miracles were also acted parables, actions that by one figure or another showed the nature of the work that he had come to do. This, the first of all of them, throws light on both the sayings quoted; for the life that Jesus came to give is as wine to water compared with anything that men had known before, and the whole purpose of his coming was to transform and complete our human nature, and with it the entire created order. But of this first miracle a narrower interpretation also is permissible. In those obedient servants, who thus eagerly, although unknowingly, supplied the raw material for his miracle, we may see a figure of the

[1] John 10.10; Matt. 5.17.   [2] John 2.1-10.

prophets and other members of the Chosen People who, guided by the Holy Spirit to ends beyond their knowledge, made ready the great theological ideas which the Old Testament enshrines, in preparation for the coming of our Lord. Of these ideas that he found ready waiting to be transfigured and fulfilled, none is more important than the idea of life. Of course to discuss this fully would need a book to itself. Here we can take only the central points.

In the first place, of course, God himself is presented as the Being supremely alive, and so the source of all created life. With this the Bible opens. All things, so we learn from Genesis, came into being at his word, and the crown of creation was man, made in his own image, made by him to be a living soul by the inbreathing of the breath of life.[1] Elsewhere in the Old Testament, however, this myth of 'creation', as it is commonly called, crops up in a much earlier and cruder form; and as this nevertheless contains some features of supreme importance we must look at it. It is not creation absolute, the bringing into being of something out of nothing, that is envisaged in this ancient tale, for that is a conception outside the range of primitive thought. What it does present is the evocation by God of the present orderly world out of prevenient chaos; and that 'creation' appears in consequence as following upon and issuing from his victory, as God of light, over the hostile darkness and disorder; it appears also as effected for the sake of man. The rhythm of the story therefore has

[1] Gen. 1 and 2.

three parts—first chaos, then the conflict between God and his enemy, lastly the cosmos, the safe and fertile earth brought from the chaos waters to be the home of man. As we know that our Pleistocene forebears, in the very areas to which this myth and those akin to it are native, experienced at least one period of terrestrial disturbance and catastrophe that must have lasted over many generations, it is reasonable to suppose that in this myth there is a nucleus of fossil history, a legendary kernel transmitted through many thousand years, embodying the memories of those survivors of the race who saw those fearful happenings yield at last, and in a way beyond all hope, to settled and serene conditions. It is noteworthy at any rate that the order of 'creation', as given even in the sublimated form of the myth in Genesis 1, exactly fits with such a period of settlement. Light appears first—a new phenomenon; then as the atmosphere clears still further with the lessening—presumably—of volcanic activity; the vault of heaven is seen again for the first time in human memory. Dry land emerges next, as the chaos waters fall, and on it vegetation quickly gains a hold. Next, in the ever-clearing sky, sun, moon, and stars appear; aquatic animals and birds begin to multiply, and after them the slower breeding land animals, and lastly man, who in this setting seems as a new creature that only now has come to be at all.

Whether we are right or not, however, in thus regarding the 'creation' myth as history in the sense that it preserves the memory of something that actually occurred, this much is certain. For the Hebrew people, it *was* history. It was the true story of what God, their God, had done 'in the beginning', and had done *for man*. And this initial act of his, which culminated in man's establishment upon a fertile, stable earth, set the pattern for his later acts. Supremely, centrally, to the eye of Hebrew faith, that pattern was repeated in the great deliverance of Israel from Egypt. The *dramatis personæ* in the two stories correspond exactly. In the beginning God's enemy was Deep—even in Genesis this is a proper name, without the article; and the beneficiary of his victory, the creature saved and made by him, was man. In the re-enaction, the enemy is at once 'Reed Sea', again a proper name in the original, and Egypt, the enslaving power, who—as we shall shortly see—elsewhere in Scripture for that reason shares with the primæval foe the name of Rahab, or 'the stormy one', and the beneficiary is Israel, the Chosen People, which in its own view is the crown of man, as man was that of all creation, Israel who is saved both from and by Reed Sea, and thereafter created the People of God by the covenant of Sinai, the People who are led thence to their promised home.

This parallel is often pointed. In Psalm 136, for instance, the Lord is praised and thanked first for his 'great wonders' in Creation (vv. 5-9), and then, in the ensuing verses, for his like wonders in bringing Israel from Egypt to the promised land. This is by implication the greater marvel of the two. And that is why, much later, when the Chosen People was once more dispossessed, we find the prophet of the Exile, whom we call Second Isaiah, addressing the Lord thus:

> Awake, awake, put on strength, O arm of the Lord!
> Awake, as in the days of old, the generations of old time!
> Art thou not he who cut Rahab in pieces, who pierced Dragon?
> Art thou not he who dried up Sea, the waters of great Deep,
> Who made the depths of Sea a way for the ransomed to pass over?[1]

You see what he is getting at. Rahab, Dragon, Deep, and Sea are proper names that cover the primæval foe and Egypt and Reed Sea. The Lord is thus reminded of both his previous mighty acts in order to incite him to a third—a third on the same pattern, and of the same kind. That means that the Lord must again engage in conflict with his People's enemy on their behalf, and win a victory which will result in their salvation and their recreation.

We have jumped on from Creation and the Exodus to this great prophecy of a third saving, recreative act of God, because the three together form the starting-point of the New Testament. But the same pattern appears in many other acts of his in the Old Testament, and some of these we find associated with the epithet 'the living God'. For instance, before the crossing of Jordan Joshua tells the people, 'Hereby ye shall know that the living God is among you.' Again, the stripling David says

---

[1] Isa. 51.9 f.

about Goliath, whose overthrow he looks to see, 'Who is this uncircumcised Philistine, that he should defy the armies of the living God?' The same idea is present, though without the epithet, in the great scene on Carmel; it is the God who acts and sends the fire from heaven in answer to the prophet's prayer, who is acclaimed '*the* God'. Much later still, Darius, convinced and awed by Daniel's preservation in the lions' den, orders his subjects everywhere to worship Daniel's God, 'for he is the living God, and steadfast for ever'.[1]

This idea that God shows his own livingness by acting to save and make the life of man crops up repeatedly. It lies behind such challenges as 'Up, Lord!' and 'Arise, O Lord!'; it also prompts such passionate interrogations as the Whys and How longs of the psalms. God is required and expected by his People to vindicate himself, to show men what he is by what he does. And what he does do is to save and to remake their *life*.

The two first things that the Old Testament teaches about life are therefore these: (1) God himself is the One supremely living, and the source of all created life. (2) God shows his livingness by saving and creative action on behalf of man.

[1] Josh. 3.10; I Sam. 17.26; I Kings 18.39 (but read the whole chapter); Dan.6.26.

The Religious Book Club

BULLETIN 134
JANUARY 1960
SCM Press Ltd
56 Bloomsbury Street
London, WC1

Dr Hugh Martin
writes about 'This is Life'

I find this a rich book, in spite of its brevity and apparent
simplicity. And it is a real book—by which I mean that it is not
remotely pious but in touch with life as you and I live it, and that
it has a firm grasp of the Christian essentials. Every now and then
it gives a pleasantly unexpected turn to the argument, and has
flashes of a pretty wit. It is intended only for the serious,
practising Christian and takes for granted that the reader is
honestly trying. To anyone in that group it cannot fail to be
helpful.

The writer belongs to an Anglo-Catholic religious community
and her idiom is not always mine, but if Free Churchmen and
Anglican evangelicals find her approach sometimes unfamiliar that
ought to be a signal to pay all the more attention, since the
chances are that we are about to learn something valuable—
though I think that occasionally we shall remain unconvinced!

The book is about the Christian life, as led by Christ himself,
and as it ought to be led by his followers. There are three good,
illuminating chapters on 'Life' in the Bible, though there is a
sense in which the whole book is about the Bible. We never get far
from it, and later chapters tell us how best to read it. (I confess her
suggestion that her 'busy' readers might pick up Hebrew, Greek

and Latin in their spare time just leaves me gaping!) Wise and experienced chapters treat of worship, corporate and private, and of the practice of the presence of God through the ordinary run of daily living.

From the Editor's Desk

Enrolling New Members

I want to say a brief 'thank you' to all of you who have responded to our appeal for new members—and particularly to those of you whose imaginative generosity has enabled us to enrol in the Club missionaries and other ministers overseas. I think it a tribute to the Club that quite a few of those who sent gift subscriptions are themselves ordained. One member who sent two gift subscriptions is a private in the army in Malaya.

During the months of January and February we offer to any Book Club member who secures one or more new enrolments a free copy of *Jesus and His Story* by Ethelbert Stauffer. Drawing new material from Jewish and Roman sources, Professor Stauffer gives us a portrait, definite, dramatic and full of fascinating detail, of a Jesus whose majesty is all the more tremendous when seen afresh against its original background. This book is being published in January in our general list, price 12s 6d.

Reaction to MacIntyre

Members seem to have found Alasdair MacIntyre's book last September easier going than I expected. A parson writes from the English Midlands: 'There were some sections one had to read a number of times, but there were those explaining philosophical methods with which I am not familiar. I much valued his honest approach. His not providing easy answers has helped me far more in facing my own doubts and problems than any other book I have come across.'

2

There is a real danger that the ecumenical movement may be perpetuated as the hobby of SCM-trained church leaders, who hop around from committee to council to conference. But the ecumenical leadership *can* talk sense to the laity; and when it does, lay people begin to recover 'the whole Christ'. At all costs, the laity must now be involved in the search for unity—by an arising on the scale of the *Kirchentag* movement, which gathers lay Germans in their hundreds of thousands. Most British efforts in this direction to date have been (although sincere) tragically inadequate. Hence, no doubt, the failure of recent summit talks between theologians!

When the Metropolitan Parthenios of Carthage declared at the WCC meeting on the island of Rhodes last August, 'For us Orthodox, the word "mission" is something which we fear', he voiced not only the fears of his particular church that Protestant missionaries may 'sheep steal' among the Orthodox faithful, but also our deepest spiritual problem. In ecumenical circles it is often said that renewal and reunion will come only through mission. I am sure that is right. But I ask: how will *mission* come? As we face the inhabited earth in 1960, *do we not need a new Pentecost?* Dr J. H. Oldham, who was Secretary of 'Edinburgh 1910', will be discussing this question in the next RBC Bulletin.

To me, these are facts. Whether or not you agree that they are (I shall be glad to hear), we shall agree on the importance of one further fact—that each year the period January 18th–25th is commended by the World Council of Churches and many Roman Catholic authorities as the Week of Prayer for Christian Unity.

D.L.E.

Many of these questions are explored fully in three new SCM Press books: The Pressure of our Common Calling *by W. A. Visser 't Hooft (12s 6d);* A Decisive Hour for the Christian Mission *by D. T. Niles and others (March 1960, 5s);* Men of Unity *by Stephen Neill (July 1960, 6s).*

The Dying and Living Lord

'Christoph Blumhardt once said that we ought to weep at Christmas, because then God is giving so much away, because God is coming into the world in sacrifice; but on Good Friday we ought to laugh; for then God is bringing the world back to Himself. And since He went down into the deepest depths, into the irrevocable hopelessness of those who are dead and buried, then "He calls into existence the things that do not exist" (Rom. 4. 17). That is the message of Good Friday.

'Henceforth from this One who was buried there falls upon our own death a great shadow and a radiant light. A *shadow*—for this we learn in the death of Jesus Christ: he who is dead is really, irrevocably, *dead*. Death in itself is not, as our poets would like to think, a fulfilment. It is a tearing away, a breakdown, a condemnation, which makes all life lose its meaning. It is "the wages of sin". A *bright light*—for here we learn for our own death, from the death of Jesus, the song of praise: "I shall not die but live." When we go into the grave with Him, with Christ Himself, we are not alone—there, where man is so utterly alone, and so lonely. One has lain before us in our own grave, and He will lift the lid and roll away the stone of hopelessness and finality. Through Him those who die do really rise again and praise God. Through Him graves really do become places where God's goodness and faithfulness are praised.'

From *The Dying and Living Lord* by Helmut Gollwitzer, 5s net. These meditations on the passion and resurrection of our Lord, now translated into English by Olive Wyon, had their origin in Dr Gollwitzer's work in Berlin during the years 1939 and 1940, when he was successor to Dr Martin Niemöller as pastor of the congregation of the Confessing Church in Dahlem.

Printed in England by Staples Printers Limited at their Rochester, Kent, establishment

3

'LIFE' IN THE OLD TESTAMENT: II

THE THIRD MAIN POINT in the Old Testament idea of
life is this: As all life comes from God, who is himself
supremely living and shows his livingness by acting on
behalf of man, so does the life of man in the full sense
consist in loving and obeying him. 'See, I have set before
thee this day life and good, and death and evil,' says
Moses to the People of the Lord in Deuteronomy, 'in
that I command thee this day to love the Lord thy God,
to walk in his ways, and to keep his commandments . . .
that thou mayest live and multiply.'[1] The predominant
Hebrew conception of judgment is the corollary of this
belief that human life consists in right relationship with
God. With us the word 'judgment' has a forensic sound;
the picture it evokes is of a court of law, complete with
plaintiffs and defendants, judge and jury. With the
Chosen People, however, judgment meant fundament-
ally God's manifestation of merit or demerit by its
recompense. He, being righteous himself, expected a
like character in those who worshipped him; only when
they too were righteous might they expect him to bless
them—that is, to make them prosperous and happy; for

[1] Deut. 30.15 f.

17

by sending them prosperity he vindicated both himself and them. Conversely, if they were disobedient, he sent them adversity.

That is the idea that runs through the Book of Judges. When Israel obeys, she prospers; when she goes after other gods, her own God allows her enemies to conquer her. Adversity, according to this view, is punitive; if you were disobedient to God's law, you asked for it, you had it coming to you, as the saying is. The same idea, applied to the individual rather than the people, but still in black and white with no half-tones, forms the theme of the first Psalm. The 'blessed' or happy man is there defined as he who keeps clear of sinners and scoffers and makes the law of the Lord his ceaseless study and joy. By a figure which spans the Bible from Genesis to Revelation, and derives ultimately from oasis memories of Israel's nomadic days, he is compared to a tree planted by the waterside, fruitful and green. But 'as for the ungodly, it is not so with them'. They have no anchorage, no water-nourished roots, no life, but are as dry and sterile as the windblown chaff. So, when the judgment comes, they cannot stand, and the path they have been following fades out—that is the basic meaning of the word translated 'perish'—leaving them in the desert, waterless and lost; whereas the Lord 'regards' the good man's way, which means he makes it his concern to prosper it, and see it through.

The stress on keeping the law in this psalm shows it to be a late one, certainly post-exilic, and on one theory it is the latest of them all, composed to form the prologue to the Psalter at its final compilation, which may have been not much more than a century before the birth of Christ. Yet, as we noted, in its insistence that happiness results from goodness—a view which on the face of it appears inadequate to cover all the facts of everyday experience—it is as clear-cut and uncompromising as is the Book of Judges. But that is not to say that Israel had made no progress in the intervening centuries. In her view of suffering and adversity she—or at least the most far-seeing of her sons—had in fact made two very great advances. Let us think briefly in this chapter what these were, and how, progressing in a spiral, as it were, they brought her round to where she started from, but on a higher plane.

In a primitive society men think of God as powerful indeed, but of uncertain temper, and as failing moreover to distinguish between inadvertent transgressions of his will and wilful ones. They are also much more conscious of belonging to the tribe or people, than of themselves as individual beings. In such a milieu, the idea of suffering as punitive is natural, and goes unquestioned. The sin of one or some involves them all, and the innocent suffer with the guilty as a matter of course. The Chosen People began on this primitive level, but they did not stop there. By the eighth century the prophets at any rate had attained an overwhelming apprehension of the holiness and righteousness of God. Isaiah of Jerusalem was one of these; the means by which his call came to him and from which his whole later work proceeded was his opening vision in the temple of the Lord 'high and lifted up', acclaimed as 'Holy, Holy, Holy' by the heavenly hosts.[1] Like Amos and Hosea and Micah in his own century, and Jeremiah in the next, Isaiah of Jerusalem saw the Exile coming as the just punishment of national apostasy; thus far all the prophets still saw adversity as punitive. But large as the impending horror loomed with them, none of them saw it as the end. They all glimpsed something of a new life beyond it; and Isaiah in particular maintained this hope with such insistence that he called his eldest son by a name that meant A-Remnant-Shall-Return.[2] That remnant would consist of the best, not the worst of the People. These would suffer the Exile, but would return eventually to refound the nation in Jerusalem.

I do not think that Isaiah or any other prophet actually says anywhere that this faithful remnant would be purged by suffering, but the idea is there. That constitutes the first of the two great advances in the Hebrew view of suffering. It is still regarded—and rightly—as punitive, as being brought upon the People by their own unfaithfulness; but its purpose in the will of God and its effect where it is taken with good will is seen as positive and as beneficent. Remembering that man's true life consists in right relationship with God, we can therefore put the new view like this: adverse and painful circumstances are potentially *good* for life, and favourable for its development. The post-exilic psalmist would admit this: 'It is good for me that I have been

---

[1] Isa. 6.   [2] Isa. 7.3.

in trouble.'[1] That goes both for the individual and for the People as a whole.

Life comes from God, who is himself supremely living. The life of man in the full sense consists in loving and obeying him. Adverse conditions, where a man can take them, as we say today, so far from hindering that life, purge and promote it. With that, the waterpot of the Old Testament idea of life is three parts full. By the end of the Exile itself, it was filled to the brim, though there were still a full five centuries before its contents could be turned to wine. The germ of the crowning spiritual discovery was latent in the previous one, but not developed. The faithful remnant, as we said, consisted of the best, and not the worst, of Israel's sons; yet they all shared the punishment of Exile, and indeed its sufferings and deprivations were more acute for these 'poor', as they came to be called, than for those less godly who cared less for what was lost and left behind. The last advance, the peak of faith's attainment under the Old Covenant, was born of the discipline of those sixty years upon the faithful few, and is embodied in the Second Isaiah's visions of the suffering Servant of the Lord.[2]

That mysterious figure appears first as the mouthpiece of God, the instrument through whom he wills both to reveal himself to the Gentiles, among whom his People then was living, and to lead back that People to himself. That is the first thing that appears about him. Secondly, the Servant fulfils this mission faithfully, but

---

[1] Psa. 119.71.   [2] Isa. 42.1-9; 49.1-6, 50.4-11; 52.13-53.12.

21

those to whom he is sent reject his message and abuse his person. He thus becomes a man of sorrows through his faithfulness, a man despised, oppressed, afflicted, and ultimately put to death. His death, though it is murder, is however something more, and made to be that something more by the Servant himself. He is 'led as a lamb to the slaughter'—that is, as a sacrificial victim to the altar, and he goes of his own will. Thus his death, although inflicted, is a willing act; in it, as priest of his own sacrifice, he makes his life an offering for the sin of those who take it away. Moreover, all this happens in accordance with the will of God. 'It pleased the Lord to bruise him; he hath put him to grief.' And why ? So that the will of God, which was the purpose of the Servant's mission, may be fulfilled not only in spite of his rejection, but by means of it. For here, where man and God alike appear to fail, man in that those whom he seeks to win reject him, and God in that he lets his Servant suffer even unto death and does not intervene, the final issue is not failure, but success, triumph beyond all thought. The Servant's pains of death turn out to be the pains of birth. The issue of it is his *seed*, the *People* ransomed by his sacrifice for God. So those who would not have the Saviour are yet saved by him. So also he himself is 'satisfied'; his joy is full, for he has done what he set out to do.

That is a summary of what the picture given in the four great Servant Songs suggests. We do not think in terms of sacrifice today; indeed the very word is so debased in common speech that its associations are rather

with the bargain basement than with the solemn inter-
course of God and man. But sacrifice in the true, ancient
sense is central in the Bible, and we have got to face it,
if we are to understand the Christian faith at all. The
point I want to make about it here is simply this: its
purpose always, everywhere, is *to give life*. 'The life is
in the blood';[1] that is a fact of common observation. So
blood is shed in sacrifice, not to destroy the victim's
life, but to set it free from its visible and earthly habita-
tion to go to the unseen God, from whom it came. As
life is the best and holiest thing that man receives from
God, it is therefore the best gift man can give to him.
As sin makes a barrier between God and man, and so
makes God withhold the blessings of life from him, man
hopes by offering life to God to make atonement for his
sins, and so renew his life supply. Bloody sacrifice is
thus regarded as the supremely efficacious means of
promoting life. It involves death, but that is not its purpose. Its aim and its result are *life*.

Those are the basic, broad ideas behind all sacrifice.
In the Suffering Servant they are particularized. The
victim is a man, and not an animal, a man obedient and
innocent, who suffers undeservedly but willingly. He is
punished not only *with* the guilty—for death is the universal consequence and punishment of sin, but on their
behalf. He, who needs no cleansing, undergoes the purg-
ing discipline. With what result? In his case, suffering
and death, the utmost sum of all adversity, *because he
makes them the material of sacrifice*, become not only

[1] Lev. 17.11.

23

punitive and purgative, but redemptive also, and creative of new life.

The Servant's story thus follows the pattern of the acts of God. As God did in Creation and the Exodus, so here the Servant comes to a chaotic scene, and there engages in a conflict with the hostile powers, of which the issue is salvation and a new creation. Thus his achievement is in fact represented as the act of God.

Now come back for a moment to Ps. 1, of which we were speaking earlier in this chapter, the psalm that draws the picture of the *happy* man. Read it, and set it by this other picture of the Servant of the Lord, whose utmost joy comes through his suffering, because he bears it willingly, and through it makes an offering of himself to God . . .

So it emerges that suffering, adversity and death are *not* inimical to the true life of man. Rather they are the very means by which that life is made, *if only they are rightly used and borne.*

With this, the waterpot of the Old Testament idea of life is filled to the brim. In the next chapter we must trace its transformation in the New.

24

4

'LIFE' IN THE NEW TESTAMENT

THE OLD TESTAMENT teaching about God is that he shows his livingness by acting and is the source of all created life, and that the true life of man consists in loving and obeying him. But all this is taught us there in bits and pieces and at different times in very various ways. The New Testament, on the other hand, presents us with all this and more summed up, concentrated, consummated in the single Person of our Lord and Saviour Jesus Christ. As the Epistle to the Hebrews puts it, 'God, who at sundry times and in divers manners spake in time past unto the fathers by the prophets, hath in these last days spoken unto *us* by his Son.'[1]

Jesus, the Word of God, the Word made flesh,[2] God's revelation of himself in terms that we can understand. You might spend your whole life thinking what this means along one avenue or other of mystery and wonder, and still have others to explore, and reach the end of none. For the purposes of this book about life for busy Christians we must, however, take just this:

In the New Testament our Lord is represented and explained as being at one and the same time Messiah,

---

[1] Heb. 1.1 f.   [2] John 1.1-14.

Suffering Servant of the Lord, and Second Adam. Let us take these in turn.

'Messiah' means 'Anointed'. In the Old Testament, as elsewhere, even in our own country to the present day, you find men made to be kings by being anointed with oil.[1] This symbolizes their endowment with divine strength for their office, and a Hebrew king was called '*the Lord's Anointed*',[2] because he was the Lord's vice-regent and vice-gerent upon earth. This point is important. In primitive thought, which so often embodies primary truth, the ultimate king is always God himself; the earthly king is such only by delegation, never absolutely. But as God's representative on earth, he is a mediator and—as such—a priest. On the one hand, he is a sacred person, called the 'son' of God, standing in a unique relation to him, and acting as his mouthpiece and his agent to the People he is called to rule. On the other, just because he is himself a man and member of the People, he stands for them to God, and they are held to be included and summed up in him; so that, if he is blessed, the People shares his blessedness, and *vice versa*. To give an instance, this is the idea behind the story in II Sam. 21.15 ff., where, when old king David's strength has failed in battle, his men declare, 'Thou shalt go no more out with us to battle, that thou quench not the lamp of Israel'—i.e. it would be all up with the People if the king was overthrown and killed. It appears again in the cry of anguish in Lam. 4.20, when the king

[1] E.g., Saul in I Sam. 10.1; David in I Sam. 16.12 f.
[2] E.g., II Sam. 1.14.

has been taken prisoner, 'The breath of our nostrils; the Anointed of the Lord, was taken in their pits.'

The priest-king was thus ideally the lamp or light of his people, because through him they got, in him they saw the light of God. He was their very breath of life, because he linked them up with God, and was the means by which their life was fed.

The king was moreover the active agent of God. When, for example, there was an enemy to meet, it was believed that God himself went out to battle for his People in the person of the king.

The Davidic kingship came to an end in the sixth century BC. But the hope of its eventual restoration, the belief that there would yet appear a son of David to sit on David's throne and reinstate his People, persisted. This expected king was called Messiah, which in Greek is Christ. There are, as you well know, many prophecies of the Messiah in the prophets. It is worth noting that one of the titles given to him by the prophet Isaiah is *Ēl-gibbôr*. This is translated 'mighty God' in our versions, but literally it is 'Hero-God'. No doubt it was taken as meaning no more than 'godlike hero', but the implication of the title is that Messiah, when he came, would act as God himself had acted in Creation and the Exodus—that is, he would engage in conflict with the hostile powers, and salvation and a new creation would be the outcome of his victory.

First the natural, then the spiritual. First the type, the outline sketch, the shadow cast before to help our understanding; then the reality foreshown. Jesus, the incarnate Son of God, who also was the Son of David according to the flesh, is shown to us in the New Testament as this Messiah. As the Messiah, the priest-king, he is his People's life, their link with God, their champion, their Saviour, their Creator.

One of the titles of the Hebrew kings was 'Servant of the Lord'. All the same, no Jew would ever have dreamed of taking Second Isaiah's vision of the Suffering Servant of the Lord as meaning the Messiah, for to them a Messiah who got put to death was quite unthinkable. But after Jesus' resurrection and ascension and the coming of the Holy Spirit, it was obvious at last to every follower of his that he was that victorious and faithful Servant, and that his death upon the cross, although inflicted by his enemies, had been in fact a willing act on his own part, the one sufficient sacrifice for human sin, which resulted in atonement between God and man and the creation of a new holy People for the Lord.

So as the Suffering Servant also Jesus is our priest and our sole source of life, but with this added, that it is by his sacrifice that we are saved, by his death that we live.

Yet our Lord never called himself either the Servant of the Lord or Son of David, although towards the end he did accept the latter title when it was given him, and did, when asked directly, acknowledge that he was the Christ.[1] The only title by which he ever called himself was 'the Son of Man'.

'The Son of Man' is an Aramaic expression that means

[1] Matt. 21.15; 26.63 f.

simply 'the Man'. It derives from a vision in the Book of
Daniel,[1] where 'one like unto a son of man' is brought
to the Ancient of Days in heaven, and given dominion
over all the earth by him. This mysterious figure is con-
trasted with the four beasts, whose power is taken
away. Daniel was written in the second century BC,
when the Chosen People were suffering desperate perse-
cution under King Antiochus Epiphanes. In its immediate reference, the four beasts stand for the four em-
pires which successively oppressed the Jews, and the
'one like to a son of man' is the People themselves, seen
as saved and given their rightful position of predomin-
ance by God, not on the plane of earthly history—for
that at this time seemed entirely beyond all hope—but
in the heavenly sphere. Alternatively, the 'one like to a
son of man' could be, and sometimes was interpreted as
an individual, a sort of superhuman, heavenly Messiah.
It was thus a Messianic title in a sense, apt for our Lord
to take because it lacked the revolutionary and political
associations of Messiah proper. But that is secondary.
The key fact about it is that it declared him, as The
Man by contrast with the beasts and having world
dominion, to be the Second Adam, the new Head of the
human race, the wellspring of its life.

The new Head, Man remade, the New Humanity.
That is what Jesus is. The perfect Man, who trusts,
loves, and obeys God perfectly, and draws his life from
him, as a green tree from the water at its roots. The
Man in whom the Fall of the first Man is reversed and

[1] Dan. 7.1-14.

its damage undone, the Man in whom the human race begins again.

This is where we come in, we busy Christians at the present day.

Our Lord told his disciples, 'I am the vine, ye are the branches.'[1] You, at your baptism, were made a branch of him; *you*, who are part of the sinful old humanity, were made part of the sinless New. That means that you live by his life and as he lives, or not at all. He is emphatic on that point; see the first six verses of John 15. Consider this.

Consider next that his own perfect human life was lived under conditions at least as hectic and exacting as your own. He was constantly thronged by demanding and often hostile people. Sometimes he had no leisure so much as to eat, no space for prayer but what he took from sleep.[2] The secret of his perfectness was simply that he—even he—as Hebrews puts it, 'learned obedience by the things that he suffered'.[3] He took what came, as from his Father's loving hand, and loved him back with it, making it the material of his sacrifice. He loved God back with every fibre of his being, with every moment of his time, with all the circumstances of his life and death.

Consider also what, the night before he died, he asked his Father for his friends:[4]

'Holy Father, keep through thine own name those

---

[1] John 15.5.   [2] Mark 6.31; 1.35.   [3] Heb. 5.8.
[4] The quotations that follow are from John 17.11-21. The whole chapter should be read.

whom thou hast given me, that they may be one, as
we are . . . I pray not that thou shouldest take them
out of the world, but that thou shouldest keep them
from the evil . . . They are not *of* the world, even as
I am not *of* the world. Sanctify them through thy
truth. Thy word is truth.'

To 'sanctify' is to make holy, and that—as we have
seen—is the meaning also of 'to sacrifice'. The Greek
word used here is used in the Septuagint in a sacrificial
connection. It is as though our Lord, on the eve of his
self-offering upon the cross, prayed for his friends,
'Make them a sacrifice too.' Then he goes on:

'As thou hast sent me into the world, even so have
I sent them into the world; and for their sakes I sanctify—make a sacrifice of—myself, that they also
might be sanctified—made into a sacrifice—through
the truth.'

Then he turns from praying for the apostolic band then
gathered with him, the nucleus of his Church, the first
extension of his Incarnation, and looks down the ages
at the 'seed' that is to issue from his travail, 'the People
that shall be born',[1] of which you and I are by his mercy
part:

'Neither pray I for these alone, but for them also
which shall believe on me through their word, that
they all may be one, as thou, Father, art in me and I in
thee, that they also may be one in us, that the world
may believe that thou hast sent me . . .'

We Christians, then, are in the world, but are not of it,

[1] Isa. 53.10; Pss. 22.31; 102.18.

31

because we are in Christ, engrafted into the New Humanity. And we, who are not of the world, are in the world *for the sake of the world*, that through us Jesus may continue his mission to it.

The Christian life, as Christ himself describes it and intends it, is thus none other than his own incarnate life in this world extended in his members who are in it now, enlightening its darkness, working like leaven in the lump of unregenerate humanity towards the final consummation of his whole saving, re-creative work. Nobody pretends that this is easy. It was not so for him, and it is both enough and fitting that the disciple should be as his Lord.[1] But what more could you, as a human person, want, what greater honour could you have, what more superb adventure could you possibly be asked to share, than to be thus taken into Christ and made his fellow-worker?

In the remaining chapters of this book we have to think a little how we can let Christ live and love God back in us, in the sundry departments and activities of daily life in this unquiet and bewildering world.

[1] In Matt. 10.25 the Greek word means 'enough'. It has however been suggested that what our Lord said was 'fitting', and that the present Greek word is due to a misreading of the Aramaic.

5

WORSHIP IN CHURCH:
1. Old and New

THE OLD TESTAMENT counterpart of our Christian 'going to church' was first and foremost attendance at the sacrificial worship in the Jerusalem temple, first at the great annual pilgrim feasts, and later every day. In addition to this, there was in later times the weekly non-sacrificial worship of the synagogue. This secondary form of worship originated with the faithful remnant during the Babylonian Exile. The sacrificial system belonged with the temple, and might not be maintained elsewhere; all that then remained to the exiles, being thus deprived, was to meet for prayer and reading of the Scriptures. After the return to Jerusalem, both these forms of worship were maintained; but, barring those sixty years in Babylon when the latter only was possible, it was never a case of either-or. The first thing always was to attend and to take part in sacrifice.

'O Lord, by these things men live: and in all these things'—or 'wholly therein'—'is the life of my spirit.'

Those are the words of Hezekiah, king of Judah, in the thirty-eighth chapter of Isaiah. Hezekiah was a descendant of David who lived in the eighth century BC. He seems moreover to have inherited something of

B   33

David's gift of psalmody, for the words quoted occur in a song which he wrote himself. The occasion which prompted him to write was this: he had fallen very ill, and the prophet Isaiah had come to see him and told him from the Lord that he was going to die. At the king's humble prayer, however, the Lord relented, and sent the prophet back to tell him that he should live another fifteen years. After his recovery, Hezekiah wrote this song as a thanksgiving. It is retrospective; he begins by describing how he felt and what he said when he believed himself about to die:

> 'I said, "In the cutting off of my days:
> I shall go to the gates of the grave" . . .
> I said, "I shall not see the Lord:
> the Lord in the land of the living." '

'To see the Lord' was the technical expression in pre-exilic times for going to Jerusalem to one of those great annual feasts. After the Exile, the Jews seem to have thought the term unsuitable; so by altering the vowels of the Hebrew word 'to see' they made it mean 'to be seen' or 'to be seen before'. In many places in the Old Testament that is the form in which it now occurs; in our versions it is mostly rendered 'to appear before the Lord'.[1] But Hezekiah had no such inhibitions. He used the original term, for when he went to worship in the temple, he did not go merely to present himself before the Lord. He went to *see* the Lord, to meet and get experience of him. So, when he thought himself about to

[1] E.g., Ex. 23.14-17; Deut. 16.16; Ps. 42.2.

die, the first thing that occurred to him was this: 'I shall never again attend the Feast of Passover, or Pentecost, or Tabernacles, to worship the Lord and have communion with him through sacrifice, in his holy city, with his holy People.' The Hebrews had at this time only a shadowy idea of life beyond the grave; a man looked to live on more in his descendants here on earth than in his personal existence there. So for this good and faithful king the central deprivation that death would entail, the thing that he would most mind leaving when he died, was sharing in those solemn acts of worship in which, as a People, Israel 'saw the Lord'. For by those things men *lived*, and wholly in them was the life of Hezekiah's spirit.

In modern parlance, therefore, it is as though his first reaction and his prime regret were this:

'Never, never shall I go to church again!'

The same spirit of devotion to the worship of the temple informs many of the psalms. Perhaps the most striking example is the eighty-seventh. As none of our versions quite brings out its meaning, we venture here upon our own translation:

'His foundation is upon the holy hills:
    the Lord loves the gates of Sion;
    more than all the dwellings of Jacob.
Glorious things are spoken of thee:
    O city of God!'

That is the first stanza. It narrates the facts: the city that the Lord has founded stands upon the holy hills;

35

he loves it more than all the other cities of his People. Glorious things are recounted concerning it. Then comes a 'selah', which means there was some sort of interruption or change in the procedure at this point— perhaps an interlude of instrumental music to key folk up to hear the 'glorious things'. The second stanza tells us what these are. In the first two verses the speaker is the Lord himself:

> 'I will make mention of Rahab and of Babylon:
>   as among them that know me!
> Behold, Philistia and Tyre, the people of Cush:
>   each one was born there!'

Then the narrative resumes, re-emphasizing what the Lord has said:

> 'And of Sion it shall be said:
>   "Each and every one was born in her,"
> and the Most High shall stablish her!
> The Lord shall reckon, when he registers the People:
>   "This one was born there!"'

'Rahab' is a name for Egypt. The meaning is that all Israel's enemies, including Egypt and Babylon who had of old enslaved her, Philistia, Tyre, Ethiopia, and every other nation too, will be enrolled and reckoned by the Lord as citizens of Jerusalem *just as fully as if they had been Hebrews born*. In other words, the Chosen People will be ultimately co-extensive with mankind.

Another 'selah' follows this amazing affirmation, as well it may, for we certainly need a pause in which to take it in. Then what? The climax, the last verse as it appears in our translations, is strictly not a verse at all. It begins with a rubric:

' "Singers and dancers"—or, "pipe-players"—alike.'

That tells you which performers now take on. The remaining words prescribe the singers' and dancers' theme:

'All my fountains are in thee!'[1]

Try now to put away the psalm you know, the psalm that you are wont to sing or say in church with such decorum and so little zest, and try to picture its original performance in the Jerusalem temple. Vocal music and perhaps instrumental too clothes the words in leaping, running melody. The lithe upspringing bodies of the dancers move in concert with it to illustrate the theme. In this way the Chosen People state the fact—and state it in thanksgiving before God—that all the things by which they live come from their chosenness. They rejoice at being the People of the Lord, the object of his love. By thanking him, they love him back, with all their heart and mind and soul and strength.

*   *   *

You will no doubt have seen long since what I am getting at, why I have quoted Hezekiah and the eighty-seventh Psalm. You know very well that the earthly holy city with its holy People typifies the heavenly, and that when St Paul, for instance, speaks of 'the Jerusalem that is above . . . which is our mother',[2] he means the

---

[1] These may have been the first words only of the song.
[2] Gal. 4.26.

Church of Christ. You, who have been baptized, belong to this Jerusalem. You can and you should say in the words of the hymn,

> '. . . of Sion's city
> I, through grace, a member am.'[1]

Very well then. It follows that this church and city is your sole source of life. Everything that, as regenerate, you have, the faith, the sacraments, the right and power to pray through Jesus Christ our Lord, you have both from the Church and in the Church. All your fountains, all your 'fresh springs', as the Prayer Book has it, are in her alone.

That is one fact. The second, its inseparable twin, is this: all that you thus have from and in the Church, you possess also *for* the Church. 'By these things men live', but 'no man liveth unto himself'[2] alone.

By 'the Church' in this context we mean the whole body of those who are baptized or otherwise in grace.[3] The Church on earth is most sorely wounded and divided; yet, because Christ is one, it has an underlying unity. Whatever part of it admitted you and with whatever part you worship now, it was to that one Church that you were admitted. To that one Church you now belong, with that one Church on both sides of the veil

---

[1] The hymn is John Newton's 'Glorious things of thee are spoken', which is based on Ps. 87.   [2] Rom. 14.7
[3] Baptism is necessary where it may be had. But, as the Church has always recognized, God is greater even than his sacraments, and is not tied to them. For instance, martyrs like our own St Alban, who suffered unbaptized, were always regarded as having been baptized in their own blood.

you worship now. You are a Christian *before* you are an Anglican, a Methodist, a Presbyterian, or whatever it may be. In this sectarian age we do need to remember this, and to make a habit of thinking of the Church, the mystical Body of Christ, in this inclusive way. In these hyper-individualistic days, we need also to cultivate the sense of belonging to the Church, of being an organic part of that great living whole, and of depending on it for our life.

Under the Old Covenant this sense was very strong. The fact of belonging to the Chosen People of the Lord was, as we have seen, a matter for exultation. We may well take a leaf from their book.

6

WORSHIP IN CHURCH :
II. The Holy Eucharist

IN THIS CHAPTER we must pursue a little further the parallel between the two Jerusalems, the two peculiar Peoples. We noted in the last that, in the elder Church, the worship whence the People drew their life was sacrificial. Put very simply, the general idea was this: God being the acknowledged Author of their life, they owed all things to him. They offered him a victim, the best of what they had, in token of this debt. The essence of the gift was the *life* of the victim, which was held to be released to go to God by the shedding of its blood. God having accepted this sacrifice, the People themselves partook of the victim's flesh, of the very gift that they had given him. He thus accepted *them*, along with their gift, and so they were brought into communion with him, all barriers removed, the holy People with their holy God. In fact, they 'saw the Lord'.

That was one point. The second one was this: that sort of worship might be offered only in the temple at Jerusalem.[1]

Thirdly, in Psalm 87 we encountered further a spirit

[1] Jerusalem finally became the single sanctuary at the time of Josiah's reformation in 621 BC.

of exultation in worship; we saw the Chosen People letting themselves go in praise and thankfulness to God. Had we had leisure to look at some more of those ancient liturgies we call the Psalms, we should have found that this was indeed the common thing. Worship both began and primarily consisted in praise and thanksgiving for the fact of God, and for his mighty works on man's behalf. Most particularly they gave him thanks for what he had done in Creation and the Great Deliverance; for, as we saw, those were the pattern acts. Petition, asking God for things, was secondary and derived. You blessed his holy name for what he had already done; after that and on the ground of it, you asked for more. Jewish worship to this day observes this order and the predominating character of praise.

Here clearly is another waterpot, whose contents have been turned to wine by Christ. The centre of our Christian worship is the Holy Eucharist, which means Thanksgiving. Our Lord Jesus Christ 'in the same night in which he was betrayed, took bread; and when he had given thanks, he brake it, and gave it to his disciples saying, "Take, eat; this is my body which is given for you. Do this in remembrance of me." Likewise after supper he took the cup, and when he had given thanks, he gave it to them, saying, "Drink ye all of this, for this is my blood of the new testament, which is shed for you and for many for the remission of sins. Do this, as oft as ye shall drink it, in remembrance of me." [1]

[1] Last part of the Prayer of Consecration in the Book of Common Prayer, based on I Cor. 11.23-25.

Twice, on the threshold of his passion, he gave God his due of thanks. He thanked him *for* the passion, because of what the passion through his own obedience would effect. For in the passion 'God was in Christ, reconciling the world unto himself'.[1] Twice also, on the same occasion, he commanded, '*Do* this, in remembrance of me.'

The Church has 'done' it ever since, and goes on doing it, though she will never fully know in this world what it is she does. She does it, and by it and the prevenient sacrament of Baptism she herself is made. She does it in remembrance of him, and remembrance—*anamnésis*—means much more than merely recalling what Christ did the night before he died, thinking ourselves back, as it were, into the upper room two thousand years ago, though that is included. It means re-presenting the whole Act of Redemption, making it again a present fact.

The *anamnésis* thus includes re-offering the sacrifice of Christ. To make that perfect offering of himself, once and for all, and by it to reverse the Fall of man, was the work that his Father had given him to do. It was the reason for his taking human flesh at all. Of that his work, he said on Calvary that it was 'finished';[2] but 'finished' does not mean that was the end of it and no more to be done. It means that his life-work was consummated by his death, and the tense of the verb in Greek denotes that the results of what was then completed are still going on. So perhaps we should not have

[1] II Cor. 5.19.   [2] John 19.30. The Greek word is *Tetélestai*.

spoken of the Eucharist as *making* the sacrifice of Calvary a present fact, for it *is* a present fact in any case. What the Eucharist does is rather to realize it and to make it operative as a present fact for those who share in it. Our Lord 'ever liveth to make intercession for' us;[1] he as our High Priest and King worships and loves the Father without ceasing with the perfect offering of himself. In the Eucharist he gives himself to us, so that we may make him *our* sacrifice, and so, presenting our unworthy selves along with him, may find acceptance for his sake with God. He further gives himself, in his character as perfect victim, to be our *food*. So he admits us into fellowship with God.

Thus in the Holy Eucharist we are connected up with the Act of Redemption that was done once for all, as with a dynamo. We are implanted into it, as grafts into the stock.

This means—among other things—that we are united with the final consummation of his work. For though from the point of view of time that is still in the future as the goal of Christian hope, it is assured by the sacrifice which Christ once offered and now for ever pleads, and is inseparable from it. In every Eucharist our Lord humbly takes the elements of bread and wine to be his body and his blood. That act is not only the pledge of his ultimate assumption of the whole created order in the new humanity and the new heaven and earth; it is also its actual beginning.

Thus past, present, and future meet in the Eucharist

[1] Heb. 7.25.

43

as in a point. It transcends time. It also transcends space. It has been celebrated at least weekly for over nineteen centuries. It is now being celebrated somewhere on the face of the globe at every moment of the day and night. Yet all these local separate celebrations of the mystery are one, because they are all participations in the one, of which our Lord himself is the unceasing Celebrant. *Where* the Eucharist is done on earth is consequently immaterial. There is no need for Anglicans to go to Canterbury, or Roman Catholics to Rome. The Christian 'single sanctuary' is in heaven, and the earthly places where the Eucharist is done are made part of heaven, one with heaven, by the act. We are reminded of this fact by the inclusion in the liturgy of the *Tersanctus*, the song Isaiah heard the angels sing before the throne of God. We worship '*with* angels and archangels and all the company of heaven'. We have a further reminder of it in the usual structure of our churches. Nave, choir, and sanctuary typify respectively the Church on earth, the waiting Church beyond the veil, and the Church in heaven. The Eucharist is celebrated at the altar, which is the focus and centre of the sanctuary, *and you go to the altar* to receive communion. You go to heaven, already here on earth, when you go to the Holy Eucharist; for in going to that you are taken into the Act in which God, who himself is Love, is perfectly loved back.

As there is one Lord, and one Eucharist, so also is there one only Church that does it. You may be the only person present there besides the celebrant; yet at the altar you do truly meet all other Christians, living and departed. There, where heaven and earth are made one by our Lord, all Christians also are in essence one in him, their superficial differences and divisions—grievous though these are—transcended in him. Potentially also, all *Man* is one in him, the whole entire human race from the first Adam on. The final consummation of his work, which is implicit in his sacrifice and guaranteed by it, fulfils the vision of the Church's eventual catholicity, which we saw embodied in the eighty-seventh psalm.

So to the altar, Christian, you must go, however difficult it may be for you to get there. It is a matter, not of being 'high' rather than 'low', or even 'church', not 'chapel', but of basic and essential Christianity that you should go, should help to 'do' the Eucharist, and should receive the holy food. It is a matter of life and death, *the* matter of life and death. For 'except ye eat the flesh of the Son of Man, and drink his blood, ye have no life in you'.[1] 'By these things men *live*.'

[1] John 6.53, but read the whole chapter, and cf. I John 5.12.

7

WORSHIP IN CHURCH:
III. The Choir Office

IN THE FIRST of our three chapters on this subject, we noted that the Jewish Church evolved a secondary form of worship, which included no sacrifices, and therefore was not restricted to the single temple, but could be carried on in any 'synagogue' or meeting-place. The Christian Church has the counterpart of this in what is called the choir office, because—not being sacrificial—it is conducted from the choir of the church, not from the sanctuary and the altar, like the Eucharist. The ingredients of this office are exactly the same as in its Jewish antecedent—*i.e.* psalms, readings from and sometimes expositions of the Scriptures, further prayers; though all of course with this great difference that we see all things as fulfilled in Christ. The Anglican form of the choir office consists of Morning and Evening Prayer, or Matins and Evensong; and nowhere in Christendom will you find a better version for the secular clergy and the people as a whole. Matins and Evensong are, however, themselves a sixteenth century abbreviation of the seven- or eightfold choir office which is still used daily in Religious communities. It is a particular function of dedicated monks and nuns to say this office.

They call it the *Opus Dei*, or 'the Work of God'. They do it day in, day out, and some of them night in and night out too, whatever they feel like, and they do it *for the Church*. They also do it for mankind. They praise and plead with God in the daily office rather as the Church's shock troops on the praying front against the powers of evil. Their whole life as Religious is ordered so that they may do this work.

We stress this point, because some of you who read this may rarely, if ever, be able to take part in the choir office at all, and others, who perhaps are pledged to say it by their ordination promises, may sometimes find their obligation a barren, burdensome, and lonely business. For such, it will be helpful to remember that this Work of God is being done, by people called by him especially to do it. There are monasteries and convents, large or small, all the world over and in most parts of Christendom. In one form or another, and in one language or another, the Work of God is as continuous as is the offering of the Holy Eucharist.

> 'As o'er each continent and island
> The dawn leads on another day,
> The voice of prayer is never silent,
> Nor dies the strain of praise away.'

So the Work of God is like an ever-flowing river, into which now this stream pours its waters, and now that, joining the master current and borne along by it. Think of that when you 'say evensong alone'. *Alone* indeed! Or perhaps you pass a convent daily on your way to work, or live where you can hear its chapel bell. There they go, at it again, those shock troops of the Church. You have no time to stop. An act of the mind, a loving wanting to join in the prayer of the Church for the Church and for all mankind is all that you can manage. But, under those circumstances, it also is enough.

You must never put this divine office, as also it is called, before the Holy Eucharist. If it is truly impossible for you to get to church for both, then always the Lord's Supper must take precedence. But attend this secondary worship if you can, and when you can, for it is very powerful and precious; and, if you cannot get to church for it, you might do worse than say it by yourself—or part of it—in conscious union with the Church.

One other point. There is a silly notion abroad at the present day that the psalms are out of date. They are not, and they never will be. They are very old, it is true. They have their roots in primitive religion, and in some cases take their origin from beliefs and practices that were already immemorially ancient when Abraham was born. Keeping the figure of trees which was implied in speaking of their roots, you might say that the seeds from which they sprang were sown in Eden by the fourfold river; but you must then go on to say that they have their tops in heaven, in the New Jerusalem. Their holiness is something quite beyond expression. In them *man* speaks to God, as he should speak, as creature to Creator. They were already hallowed by long use when our Lord found and took them, more waterpots of Cana awaiting his transforming touch. He himself used them, not only in the synagogue and temple, but in his private prayers. Two of his seven last words from the cross are psalm quotations,[1] which shows that he was steeped in them, for dying men do not compose new prayers. He also saw himself as foreshown in the psalms, as well as in the prophets and the law,[2] and he explained himself in terms of them.[3]

His prayer-forms, one would think, are good enough for us, but that is not to say the psalms are easy. They do not yield their treasures to the superficial, nor to the lazy-minded. If you want to get inside them, you must use them, and use them with the Church, and for the Church and the whole human race.

[1] Matt. 27.46, from Ps. 22.1; Luke 23.46, from Ps. 31.5.
[2] Luke 22.44.   [3] See e.g. Matt. 21.15 f. and 22.41-45.

8

WORSHIP IN PRIVATE:

1. The Starting-Point

'O little lark, you need not fly
To seek your Master in the sky,
    He treads our native sod;
Why should you sing aloft, apart?
Sing to the heaven of my heart;
    In me, in me, in me is God!

'O strangers passing in your car,
You pity me who come so far
    On dusty feet, ill-shod;
You cannot guess, you cannot know
Upon what wings of joy I go,
    Who travel home with God.'

That is the song of a communicant trudging home from church.[1]

'*In me is God*.' Those four words state one half of the central fact of Christian life, the fact from which all else proceeds. Its other half is this: as a communicant, and even as baptized, '*In God am I*', because I am in Christ.

'Ye are the body of Christ,' says St Paul, 'and mem-

[1] 'A Basque Peasant returning from Church', by Anna Bunston (Mrs de Bary), in *The Oxford Book of Mystical Verse*, p. 589.

bers in particular.' And in another passage, 'We are
members of his body, of his flesh and of his bones.'[1]

'I am the true vine,' says the Lord himself, 'and my
Father is the husbandman. Every branch in me that
beareth not fruit he taketh it away; and every branch
that beareth fruit, he purgeth it, and it may bring forth
more fruit . . . Abide in me, and I in you. As the
branch cannot bear fruit of itself, except it abide in the
vine, no more can ye, except ye abide in me. I am the
vine, ye are the branches. He that abideth in me, and I
in him, the same bringeth forth much fruit; for without me ye can do nothing.'[2]

And again, speaking to his Father:

'I pray . . . that they all may be one, as thou, Father,
art in me, and I in thee, that they also may be one in
us; that the world may believe that thou hast sent me.

'And the glory which thou gavest me I have given
them, that they may be one, even as we are one; I in
them, and thou in me, that they may be made perfect
into one, and that the world may know that thou hast
sent me, and hast loved them, as thou hast loved me.'[3]

Earlier in the same chapter, already speaking to his
Father, he gives this definition:

'This is life eternal, that they might know thee, the
only true God, and Jesus Christ, whom thou hast sent.'[4]

Every human being is what is called in Latin *capax
Dei*, capable of God, able to receive and know him.
Every human being, not just one here and there; for it

[1] I Cor. 12.27; Eph. 5.30.   [2] John 15.1-5.   [3] John 17.20-23.
[4] John 17.3.

51

is this capacity that makes a being human. The power
is innate in every member of our race; it is that crowning gift which differentiates us from the lower creatures. And the *life* of every human being, according to
the teaching of our Lord that we have quoted, consists
in using this divinely given power of laying hold of
God, and realizing and developing this inborn capacity
for knowing him.

In this chapter we have to consider our private
prayer and worship as a means to this end. 'Private'
prayer is commonly so called to distinguish it from the
public, official worship of the Church in church. It is
'private' prayer when you drop into a church for a spot
of quiet in the dinner-hour, or when you kneel down in
your room at home, or when you lift your heart to God
in the midst of work, without any outward indication
that you are praying at all. But private prayer is never
lonely prayer. Whenever, wherever, and however you
pray, you pray with the Church and in the Church. When
we were speaking of the *Opus Dei*, we used the figure of
a river fed by streams. That river really is the prayer of
Christ himself, his ceaseless mediation between us and
God. All Christian prayer—that is, all prayer made
either to him or through him to the Father and the Holy
Spirit—becomes part of his prayer, part of that mighty
river. We need to remember this tremendous fact, and
to affirm it by repeated acts of faith.

Yet the fact that no one ever prays alone is only one
side of a paradox. All prayer is corporate—in that fact
lies the antidote to all our loneliness and sense of isola-

tion. All prayer is also individual. At the Holy Eucharist, which is the act of the Body of Christ in union with her Head, communion is given to the individual, within the Church. The words of administration in their Anglican form begin with a prayer for the individual:

'The body of our Lord Jesus Christ,
  which was given *for thee,*
The blood of our Lord Jesus Christ,
  which was shed *for thee,*

} preserve *thy* body
and soul unto
everlasting life.'

Then follow two pairs of commands, also addressed to the individual person who receives the sacrament: First, with the host:

'Take and eat this, in remembrance that Christ died *for thee.*'

Then, with the cup:

'Drink this, in remembrance that Christ's blood was shed *for thee.*'

Lastly, in the first case,

'and feed on him in thy heart by faith with thanksgiving.'

In the second, simply

'and be thankful.'

Consider the bearing of these words on private prayer.

The first point made in them is that the purpose of my reception of the sacrament is the preservation of *my whole personality,* body as well as soul or spirit, unto everlasting *life.*

The second point is that I *take* it, with my hands and

53

with my lips. It is not forced on me, nor is it instilled into me by some process or at some time unknown to me. I take it with my body and by a deliberate act of my own will. My body and my soul, which are to be preserved by it unto the everlasting life, co-operate to take it. I know both what I do and when I do it.

The third point is that I take it *into* my body, and also into my soul. This Food, which is my Lord, the Son of God made man, is at once bodily and spiritual, like myself. It matches me, and meets my need all round. But in its two aspects it operates in opposite ways. The earthly substances of bread and wine, which I receive, nourish my body and go to form its tissues, as does all my earthly food. But the body and blood of Christ, which these terrestrial elements convey to me, make *me* become part of *him*. Receiving his life, I am assimilated to it. It makes me become what I am, a member of his Body. That is what it is for.

So, in order that this marvellous and blessed process of salvation may go on in me to its appointed end, after I have received him I must go on feeding on him in my heart, by faith, and with thanksgiving. Returning from communion, in very truth I 'travel home with God'. I bring him home with me; I take him with me wherever I subsequently go. The function of my private prayer is to maintain that fellowship with him, who is at once my Guest, my Saviour, and my God.

9

WORSHIP IN PRIVATE:
II. Set Times

WE HAVE ESTABLISHED that the starting-point and *raison d'être* of Christian private prayer is the fact that the one who prays is a communicant. If the life given at baptism and at the altar is to be maintained, it must be fed by prayer. For prayer, therefore, times must be set apart, but that is not enough. We have also to learn to pray in between times, both in and *with* our other occupations. In this chapter we will think about set times.

In a busy life these are generally hard to get. But they must be got. We should regard it as a matter of life and death to get them, for that is what it literally is. And the getting of them *ought* to cost us something in the way of discipline; we should not offer to the Lord our God of that which costs us nothing. Further, we should make these times of prayer a matter of rule, not just of chance or inclination, both of which are all too liable to fail; but the rule itself must be born of prayer, or it will not get us far. This is a vital point. Other people, if they pray themselves, and know you and your circumstances well, may be able to give you good advice as to how you can make time for prayer; and both people and books can sometimes help you with your actual praying. But in the last resort it is your rule, your prayer, your capacity for God and life in him that has to be developed by your prayer, and your responsibility to God for using to the full what he has given you. You must find out what God wants you to do, and how he wants it done, and when he wants it changed, from God himself. Souls are not mass-produced; each is unique. Within the one great road that is man's life with God there are many different ways of prayer and all of them well trodden. And within these again, and weaving in and out of them with no two quite alike, there are as many individual tracks as there are individuals who pray. So pray about your rule of prayer, 'What shall I do, Lord?'[1]

For what God requires of you in the matter of prayer, as also in its manner, is ultimately secret between him and you. In the guidance that he waits to give you now there sounds in fact his earliest whisper of the 'new name' that he has promised to everyone who overcomes;[2] and that name will be known to none except yourself and him.

* * *

Suppose now that the question of times is settled. The first great difficulty in your busy life has been surmounted. Morning, midday, and evening, a little space is clear, a chance to fill your spiritual lungs, to slake your thirst at the fresh springs of God. Then, very ofen,

[1] Acts 22.10.   [2] Rev. 2.17.

comes another difficulty. Tiredness, nervous and physical exhaustion; along with them, distaste, disinclination, sheer inability to fix one's mind, apparent lack of all capacity or desire for God, resulting sometimes in a sense of reprobation. It is not always like that, but sometimes it is. That state of affairs is something that everyone experiences at times, and everyone therefore must be prepared for it and learn to deal with it.

Go back to the words of administration at the Holy Eucharist. The first point there was that the life of Christ then given was given to and for the whole of you. Your body and your soul together receive and are to live by it for ever, first on this present plane of life, then on a higher. 'Body' is the physical part of you; 'soul' covers both the intellectual and the spiritual, for man, like his Maker, is a trinity. Very well then. Since they are destined to be one to all eternity, body, mind, and spirit must all be exercised in prayer, because by prayer their joint eternal life is fed. Under the conditions that we have envisaged, the villain of the piece is body. 'I' am exhausted and—as I think—incapable of prayer, in the first place because my body is. Body, which now is hindering me from prayer, must therefore learn to help, and that not least in its own interest. How is it to be taught?

To start with, you must make it do the things that go with prayer and are its proper share. You must kneel down, because that attitude betokens the submission of man to his Maker which is implied in prayer. Our Lord

57

himself knelt in Gethsemane to pray;[1] in your own hour of distress you may call that to mind.

Your knees subdued, the next thing is your hands. Millions of Christians use their right hand first to cross themselves—that is, to make the sign of our redemption on their bodies from brow to breast, and then across the breast from left to right. It is strange that this practice of making the sign of the cross should ever have come to be regarded as 'Popish' or a party badge; one would have thought that, if there was anything all Christians held in common, then that thing was the cross. It was possibly not quite the earliest Christian symbol; the fish, with its more cryptic Christian reference,[2] may have preceded it. But it was certainly a token of the faith within forty years of the crucifixion, for by then a slave had cut it in the wall of his room in Pompeii; there it still stands, above the desk at which he said his prayers, uncovered only in this century from the volcanic ash in which Vesuvius buried that unhappy city in AD 79.[3] That man might easily have

[1] Luke 22.41.   [2] The fish was probably a Christian symbol in the first place because our Lord himself adduced 'the sign of the prophet Jonah'—i.e., his re-emergence from the belly of the 'great fish'—as a type of his resurrection. Further, *ichthus*, the Greek word for 'fish', came to be taken as an acrostic:

I Iesous = Jesus
CH Christos = Christ
TH Theou = of God
U (h) Uios = Son
S Sōtēr = Saviour

[3] See *The Destruction and Resurrection of Pompeii and Herculaneum*, by Egon Caesar Cone Corti (Routledge and Kegan Paul, 1951), pp. 41 and 208 f., and plate 19, opposite p. 116.

been converted by St Peter or St Paul, for they were martyred—St Peter on a cross—not earlier than AD 64.

Most Christians also are signed with the cross at baptism, though it is not essential that they should be so. For such, crossing themselves is a reminder that they were baptized into Christ's death, as St Paul puts it, and signifies their ratification of what was then done to them. It thus goes with that other manual act of *taking* the sacrament at the Holy Eucharist, which is commanded in the administration. The holding out of the hands and the sign of the cross alike denote the individual's acceptance of the cross, with all that the cross means. Even the sheer name and shape of the cross are tremendously significant, if you stop to think. There is the upright, running straight heavenward from earth; that stands for human life, and all created life along with it, before the Fall. Then comes the other crossing it, cutting right across its path, blocking, frustrating it; that of course is the Fall. But that is not the end. Precisely *through* the cross, through having something it must overcome, the heavenward line goes on, according to God's plan. Love makes the evil the means of its own overthrow; that is the method of divine redemption as set forth by the cross.

So there is nothing superstitious or magical about crossing oneself, nor has it reference to any unprimitive accretion on the Christian faith. The fact of our redemption through the cross of Christ was central from the first in Christianity; to make the sign of it is simply to remind yourself that through the cross you are in fact 'a member of Christ, the child of God, and an inheritor of the kingdom of heaven', with all that is entailed by that, alike of privilege and of responsibility. You may well find help in using the sign of the cross, but your hands have other things to do in prayer as well. They must be put *together*. Why?

In feudal times, when lords did homage to the king, they knelt before him with their hands together palm to palm; and, as the vassal spoke his oath of loyalty, the king enclosed his hands between his own.[1] The action meant on the one side, 'I am your man; all that I have and own is yours,' and on the other, 'I accept you wholly.' So you, by putting your hands together when you pray, declare that you belong to God, and hold all that you have and are both from and for him.

As to your eyes, there are two courses open. You can shut them, as we were taught to do as little children, so as to shut away the things of everyday and turn your inward gaze on God alone. Or you can fix them on some object of devotion, a picture or a crucifix, to help you fix your thoughts. You obviously can't do both at once, but you can ring the changes on them, according to your need.

By kneeling down, by making the sign of the cross, by putting your hands together and controlling your eyes, you have acknowledged yourself God's creature, child in

[1] This still takes place at the coronation of our own sovereign.

Christ, and dedicated servant. The prayer of your heart, for which you thus prepare, *must match the actions and the posture of your body*. That is, it must consist in the aligning of your will with God's, and not—emphatically not—in trying to get what *you* want from him. To want what he wants, whatever it may be, however difficult and hard to understand, because he wants it, is to love him back; and holiness consists in doing that. 'The only thing I want,' wrote Charles de Foucauld, 'is to do what most pleases him.' You can set your *will* to that, as you can set your body to its knees by act of will, when your feelings, which you can't control at will, are in a state of chaos. If you do set your will to it, it will wobble a lot, of course, just as a compass needle wobbles in the attempt to settle on the pole. But if you persevere you will find peace, *and you will not find peace in any other way*.

That attitude of wanting what God wants and waiting on his will is prayer; and it brings peace even when surface things are in a tumult, because a person in that attitude to God is making sense, and doing what he was created for. We, being the poor creatures that we are, however, have to establish and maintain that attitude by frequently repeated acts of prayer, of different kinds. We ought to have a scheme for our set times of prayer that includes in some form, however brief, specific acts of adoration, confession, thanksgiving, and lastly supplication—that is, petition for oneself and intercession on behalf of others. It has often been remarked that the word ACTS is made up of the initial letters of those four kinds of prayer, which helps us to remember what they are. In the last chapter we suggested that the private prayer of the communicant was covered by the charge to feed on Jesus in his heart 'by faith with thanksgiving'. Write

AC **T** S

like this, with the T covering and linking up the other letters, and you get a symbol of the truth of this. The T stands for express thanksgiving, thanking God for what he gives and does. But, when I adore him, I am still thanking him, for then I bless and give him thanks for being what he is. Again, when I confess my sins and need to him, I do so knowing not only that he will forgive and help me, but that I owe it to his love and grace that I am penitent and anxious for his help at all. So my confession, like my adoration, is shot through with thanksgiving, and indeed *is* thanksgiving in another form. Lastly, my supplication rests on the same knowledge of his love, for me, and all mankind, and all creation; and how can anybody know that love and not give thanks for it? So all my prayer, whatever form it takes, is feeding on my Saviour in my heart by faith and with thanksgiving. *Feeding*, so that his life in me and mine in him may grow, and be maintained, and what a life that is!

We have spoken so far only of private prayer with words, and mostly of our own approach to God by means of it. But not all prayer requires words, by any means, and really to put our approach to God in the first place would be to put the cart before the horse. 'We love him, because he first loved us.'[1] A great deal of our private prayer, as Christians who have received the revelation of his love, ought to consist in simple, thankful recognition of that fact, in letting him love us. This spiritual sun-bathing is vital for our soul's health. The all-too-common notion that 'contemplation'—for that is what it is—is something of which only a few chosen souls are capable is a most deadly error. As has been said, *every* human being is 'capable of God', and what does that mean but that he is able to know and to receive him, to look at him, and know himself beloved, and so to love him back? And what is that, if not to contemplate? It is precisely because we do not practise this simplest of all forms of prayer that many of us are so joyless and so ineffective, so overburdened, and so tied up with ourselves.

Go on then, busy Christian, with your private prayers. Believe in yourself, in the capability that God has given you to use and to develop, and in his love for you. Be simple and straightforward with him in your prayer. When things are difficult and you feel all a mess, just tell him all about it. If you can get the privacy, it helps sometimes to speak aloud to him in doing this, especially when one has secret fears that one is loath to face and own. Even forming the words, without saying them aloud, is more relieving than just thinking them. And when you have done all you can to get things off your chest to him, just rest in him.

[1] I John 4.19.

This is Life

'The waves of the sea are mighty, and rage horribly:
but yet the Lord, that dwelleth on high, is mightier.'[1]

The abyss may yawn, but 'underneath are the everlasting arms'.[2]

[1] Ps. 93.5.   [2] Deut. 33.27.

IO

WORSHIP IN PRIVATE:
III. Bible Reading

IN THE LAST CHAPTER we decried the common notion that contemplation is beyond the powers of all except the chosen few, and simply is not meant for busy Christians. We called it a deadly error, because by making ordinary people think such prayer is not for them, it keeps them from exercising their full capacity for God, and stunts their spiritual growth. A deadly and dangerous error it certainly is, but it does not stand alone. It has a twin, as deadly as itself. That twin is the idea that confirmation classes or the instruction that he gets in Sunday school give a person all the knowledge of the faith that he will ever need.

Put baldly like that, the absurdity of the idea is patent. No one would think such teenage knowledge adequate in any other field. But in practice many people do in fact behave as though they thought they had no more to learn. They read no books about the faith. They hardly read that book of books, the Bible.

The Bible is long. The Bible is difficult. Nevertheless the Bible is the Word of God, the Word of life. It is God's gift to us, and to accept and use it is an essential part of the worship that we owe to him. We have *got* to

read it, however busy we are. If we do not, we shall
stagnate. It will be disastrous for ourselves in any case,
if that occurs. If in any capacity we have to teach the
faith to others, it will be disastrous for them too; for we
shall have little of any worth or interest to give them.
Even those who do no formal teaching are liable to be
faced at any time with questions about what they believe and why, and such precious opportunities of witness the stagnant Christian will not have the power to
meet. It is only in so far as our own apprehension of the
truth is living and progressive that we can possibly put
it across effectively to others. So in this chapter and the
next we must think about the theory and practice of
Bible reading in a busy life.

As to the theory, first let us clear our minds as to
what the Bible is, and what we mean by saying that it
is 'inspired'. We call it the Word of God, and we apply
the same name to our Lord. The reason for this dual
usage is not far to seek. Speech expresses mind; it re-
veals what the speaker thinks, and so establishes com-
munication between him and the one addressed. Our
Lord Jesus Christ, the Son of God and Second Person of
the Blessed Trinity, is the perfect and complete expression of the mind of God. He is the *Word* of God, first
as the Agent of creation, and then because in him as
Man God speaks to men, and speaks in language they
can understand. As we have already noted in an earlier
chapter,[1] the Epistle to the Hebrews begins with an
asseveration of that fact:

[1] See p. 25

'God, who at sundry times and in divers places spake in time past unto the fathers by the prophets, hath in these last days spoken unto us by his Son . . .'

The writer is here contrasting two revelations. The first was complex, given in bits and pieces through many individuals and over a long period of time; and yet it was not full. The second, given at one time to the writer's own generation and so to all that follow, was simple, single and complete. The rest of the Epistle is devoted to showing that these two revelations, for all their difference and for all the latter's infinite superiority, are really one, because it is one God who is revealed in them. The first, the revelation to and through 'the fathers in time past', prepared for and foreshadowed that through Christ. The former Word of God was the Latter's foundation; the revelation that God made through him began where the other left off. As the Word of God, our Lord subsumes and consummates and gathers into one all that God had ever 'said' before.

Now what we rightly call 'the Bible' or THE Book, because there is none other to compare with it, is simply the written record of this revelation of himself that God the Creator has made to his creature man. The Old Testament embodies that which was given to 'the fathers' in very various degrees and ways, up and down the centuries before Christ came. The New Testament gives us in the Gospels the story of his incarnate life on earth; the Acts tells us of its continuance through the Church; and the Epistles and Apocalypse both illuminate this story on its historical side, and show how the

Church of those first days interpreted the revelation, the Word of God, that Jesus is. These two Testaments make up the one Bible, the one written Word of God. In a sense, the single subject of this written or enscriptured Word is the Word made flesh; for he is central in it, and every part of it contributes to the understanding of him in some way.

That, then, is what the Bible is, the written record of God's progressive revelation of himself, that Christ completed and summed up. Now for the question of its inspiration by the Holy Spirit. It is of faith for Christians that the Holy Spirit 'spake by the prophets'. We tend to think of a prophet as a person who foretells the future; but that is only by the way. The primary function of a prophet of God is to *forth*tell. He is the agent of God's revelation, in that he utters and declares to other men what God makes known to him; and what God tells him is not necessarily concerned with what is going to happen in the future, though it may be so. In that context—i.e., in the Nicene Creed—'the prophets' covers all the people who took any part whatever in receiving and passing on the revelation embodied in the Bible. The number of those is of course beyond all calculation. Apart from direct authors, of whom there were not a few, there must have been thousands of people who helped to formulate, preserve, and transmit the oral material on which the records rest. There must have been thousands more who were compilers, copyists, and editors. By all these the Holy Spirit 'spake'. He inspired or breathed into all of them. He is thus ultimately the Author of the Bible. It is that over-arching, single authorship *by God* that makes the Bible holy; it is that also which, together with its single subject, makes it one.

Remembering that, you must remember also that human free will is the gift of God, which he will never violate or take away. In 'speaking' by all those people, the Holy Spirit never forced their will, neither did he override the limitations due to their environment. The Bible is full of evidence both of that freedom to continue themselves on the writers' part, and of their limitations; and in the last half-century so much has been made of it and of other alleged blemishes in Holy Scripture, that people have acquired an uneasy feeling that the Bible has become discredited. As a matter of fact, within the last few years the tide has turned again. Recent discoveries in archæology and anthropology have demonstrated the historical authenticity of both Testaments in countless details that were previously scouted by the critics. Again, at the International Conference on the Four Gospels, which was held at Oxford in September, 1957, the upshot of one paper after another on questions of authenticity and authorship was an almost unqualified reversion to the positions our forefathers held, before the Higher Criticism was born. All the same, the uneasy feeling remains, and it still frightens people off the Bible. They feel—and fear —they can't depend on it, they can't accept it, as their grandparents did, unquestioningly as the Word of God. They feel this is a pity, since the old folk obviously got

This is Life

so much from it. But they are sure that they themselves have not the time or brains for serious study, such as appears to be required today if one is to get profit from the Bible, so they are forced—or think they are—to leave the thing alone.

There is here some muddled thinking to tease out, and a nettle to grasp. We have seen that the Bible, the enscriptured Word of God, is at once a divine book and a very human one; and it is that patent humanness that makes a stumbling-block for some. But we should remember that the Word made flesh also is at once divine and human. He is almighty God; yet when he was on earth his human nature, for all its sinlessness, shared the limitations not only of that nature generally in its terrestrial stage, but also of the time and place in which he lived. For instance, critical research has made it obvious to us today that the first five books of the Old Testament, which constitute the Jewish Law, are complex compilations, only the nucleus of which can be attributed to Moses, the first giver of the Law. First century Jews, however, believed that Moses wrote it all; so in the Gospels we find that our Lord speaks of 'Moses' when he means the Law.[1] That is a mark of human limitation, certainly, and we must bow before the wonder of the divine humility that came down so low; but it is NOT an error. It does not foster nor proceed from any false idea of God. In consequence, it simply does not matter. What does matter is that through that limited, restricted manhood of our Lord, God spoke. So

E.g. John 7.19.

is it with the Bible. God speaks in it, through human minds and lips; and it is for his message that we have to listen and to look. All else is by the way.

We need further to remember that all those individuals through whom the Holy Spirit got the Bible made, were members either of the Jewish or of the Christian Church; and that both in its every part and as a whole that Book, thus written by and in the Church, was also written *for* it. That does not mean that nobody outside the Church could or should ever read it. It simply means that, since the Church preceded and begat the Bible under both covenants, it is only within the Church —that is, within the Church of Christ on which the Holy Spirit came at Pentecost—and by members of the Church who are holding the faith and living the life required by the Church, that it can be rightly used and understood.

Further, members of the Church are pledged as regards the Holy Spirit not merely to believe that he exists, but to believe IN him. That means to trust him, as being what our Lord said he was, the Spirit of truth, sent by the Father to guide us who are in the Church into all the truth. The whole idea of 'truth' throughout the Bible is *that-on-which-you-can-depend*. So when you say in the Creed that you believe *in* him who spake by the prophets, you are asserting your belief that the Bible does in fact contain the very truth of God, that it is indeed his 'Word', and as such utterly dependable. That profession of faith is not compatible with the uncertain and distrustful attitude towards the Bible, of which we spoke just now. That attitude and Christian loyalty just don't agree.

There is yet another thing to be remembered, another thing that follows from the fact that the Bible is the Church's Book. The Church is the special—though not the only—sphere of the operation of the Holy Ghost today. He who spake by the prophets is given to each admitted member of the Church as fully and as certainly as he was given to the first Christians on the Day of Pentecost. You are yourself indwelt by him by whom the Bible is inspired. He, then, must link you on to it. Through and in you here, he must as it were join hands with himself there. *It rests with you* to establish this connection, to surrender yourself wholly to his guidance in your Bible reading, as in your whole life. When people find the Bible boring, it is because they have omitted to do this. They have got the power plug, and the electric heater; but they have omitted to plug the heater in and to turn on the switch. In consequence, the stove continues cold.

II

WORSHIP IN PRIVATE:
iv. Bible Reading, *continued*

WHEN WE WERE TALKING about prayer in general, we stressed the fact that no two souls pray quite alike, and that each one therefore ought to try to find how God would have him pray; and that was tantamount to saying that we should try to be extremely sensitive to God the Holy Spirit. The same applies to Bible reading, which is a form and part of prayer. So this chapter will be devoted to a few practical suggestions about how this may be done; but these must not be taken as laying down the law. It is for you to find out from the Holy Spirit how far they meet your need, and may be practicable in your case.

One needs to see the Bible first as a unity, the wood before the trees that make the wood.[1] Reference has been made already both to its single theme, and to its ultimately single authorship. You could summarize the theme in three words, Creation, Counter-Creation, Re-Creation. The first two are covered by Genesis 1-3,

[1] I tried to do this in my own first book, *The Wood: an Outline of Christianity*, first published by Heffer in 1935. This includes a survey of Church history, and in 1960 is being republished by the Faith Press, under the title of *The Wood for the Trees*.

which means that the whole of the rest of the Bible is concerned in one way or another with the last. Alternatively, you can think of it as a love story, complete with the three basic characters that we expect a love story to have; for that is what it is quite plainly shown to be. 'God so *loved* the world, that he gave his only begotten Son . . . that the world through him might be saved.'[1] God himself is the hero and lover, man is the beloved, the villain is the enemy who seeks to separate the lover from his love and ruin her. Man makes a sorry heroine, a quite unworthy bride; but the hero's love is such that he finds a way to overthrow the enemy and make her worthy of himself at last.

However one thinks of it, it does help to have the central theme always in mind; and it does help to have in one's head just the bare outline of the main periods of biblical history. The best way to get a grasp of this—at least in my experience—is to get it down on paper in the form of a time-chart. Many years ago, when I was teaching both divinity and history, we had a beauty, that ran for over sixty yards down the whole length of the school corridor. It was made of cartridge ceiling paper ten inches in depth,[2] and it ran on the scale of a yard to a century from 4000 BC to AD 2000 with a foot or two blank at each end to remind us that the period charted was after all only a section of the time between Eden and the New Jerusalem. I think we had some early Egyptian history in the fourth and third millennia BC,

[1] John 3.16.
[2] The roll was 30 in. in width, and we cut it into three.

74

as well as Noah's flood in the former. In any case, Old Testament history began firmly with Abraham, early in the second; then, following the dates most generally accepted, we had the period of the patriarchs, the sojourn in Egypt, the Exodus and the wilderness period, the Settlement in Canaan and period of the Judges, the Monarchy, the Divided Kingdom, with the fall first of Samaria, then of Jerusalem, the Babylonian Exile, the Return and Restoration, and the last bleak five centuries of hope deferred that intervened before the Incarnation, the prophets and other outstanding figures being indicated where they came. The crucial, central, infinitely consequential period of the Incarnate life on earth came next, followed by the main periods of Church history down to the present day. Below these periods of sacred history we indicated the best known of those in secular history. The children loved correlating their history and divinity like this, and seeing where their favourite characters came in. We always impressed upon them that, though our 'River of Time' ended at AD 2000, they must see it mentally as sweeping on towards the Final Consummation.

I have described this chart in detail, because if any teachers read this book, they may be moved to make one like it. But you can have a very useful chart for personal use, though with less detail, on a scale of an inch only to the century, on a strip only three inches wide and three and a half feet long, and beginning only at 2000 BC. It makes it clearer to see as a whole if you tint the periods in different colours. Along with the chart, you need an outline map of the ancient Mediterranean world and Middle East.[1]

When you have got your outline, of course you want to fill it in, and this you must do by degrees. Some people will follow the old way of reading the Bible through from Genesis to Revelation. The advantage of that method is that you do read it all, that it puts you in the way of acquiring the sort of loving familiarity with the sacred words of Scripture that the fathers and mediæval people like St. Bernard, and even our own parents and grandparents had. That familiarity is a most precious thing, and worth a lot of trouble to acquire. The Bible as a whole is fragrant with the Holy Spirit; he who inspired its writing still is present in it, as in a sacrament. There is in consequence a sort of magnetic affinity between different passages, though these are scattered up and down the Bible in very various contexts and connections. You read a verse in a prophet, perhaps, and—*if* you know your Bible—half a dozen others jump to meet it, corroborating and illuminating. The way this happens is most wonderful and most delightful, as many can testify. But it cannot happen unless you know your text. On the other hand, reading the Bible straight through has certain difficulties. First, there are long sections the relevance of which to the

---

[1] J. H. Breasted's *Ancient Times: A History of the Ancient World* (2nd ed., largely rewritten, Ginn, 1944) has excellent maps, is superbly illustrated, and makes fascinating reading as a background for all periods of biblical history. *The Westminster Historical Atlas to the Bible* (SCM Press, London, and Westminster Press, Philadelphia) is also most valuable.

main theme is not immediately apparent—Proverbs and the other Wisdom books, for instance, and the long legal codes in Exodus and in Leviticus. Reading these, one is liable to forget the central theme and get bogged down. Second, there are often duplicate versions of a narrative like those in Kings and Chronicles, or even two conflated in one text, as in the Joseph stories; and this is most confusing. What seems to be needed here, as a preparation for reading the whole Bible but most emphatically not instead of it, is a *selection* of sections, giving the essentials of the consecutive story and the developing revelation that went along with it.

This need I myself long felt acutely. Some years ago I tried to meet it in a book called *They Shall Be My People*.[1] This consists of thirty-three short plays, meant not for acting but for reading in class, or study group, or round the fire, or by the individual alone. These form a connected sequence that takes you right through the Bible from Abraham, with a backward look to Creation and the Fall to point his meaning, to St John on Patmos seeing the end of the story of God's love for man—the end that after all is only the beginning—in the final consummation of Creation and Redemption in the New Jerusalem. References are given to all the passages of Scripture from which the plays are drawn. If any readers of this book should find them helpful, the author would be very glad.

Suppose now that you have acquired, by whatever

[1] Published in two volumes by OUP in 1952. There is also a small teacher's *Handbook to the Plays*.

means, a general conspectus of the whole Bible story. You know the order of the periods and their chief events on both sides of the central happening of the coming of the Son of God in flesh. In regard to the Old Testament, you know where people like Moses, David, Elijah, Hezekiah, Zerubbabel and Jeshua, and even Antiochus and Judas Maccabaeus, come into it, and why they are important. You have a bowing acquaintance also with the writing prophets. It may be that you are beginning also to have some idea as to when and how the different books assumed their present form. In regard to the New Testament, you know the Gospels pretty well, and Acts. You know enough of the Epistles to love certain parts, such as I Corinthians 13 and 15 and Romans 8, exceedingly. You have at least read the Book of Revelation, which certainly baffles you, but we hope fascinates as well. Over the whole field of Scripture you are beginning—but only beginning—to get that loving familiarity with its holy words, of which we spoke just now.

Thus in terms of the metaphor used earlier in this chapter you have now walked right through the wood by the main track, noting the trees you passed, and the side-tracks, and having always in mind as you proceeded the vision of the lay-out of the wood, as seen whole from the air. You are however still very far from knowing the wood thoroughly, as from the ground. So the question now arises, what shall you do next? There are innumerable trees of many kinds, and countless paths between them that you might explore. Which tree shall you sit under first? Which sweet fruit shall you pluck? In which direction shall you walk from one tree to the next?

The answer of course is, you must proceed as you are led. A person who wants to be obedient to the Holy Spirit in his Bible reading will not lack for *attraits* in respect of it, and these should be pursued with zest. We offer here a few suggestions about means and methods.

First there is the question, 'What version shall I read?' For sheer beauty of language the Authorized Version of 1611 is the best any day. No other is so easy on the ear and tongue, none reads aloud so well. It is most precious, but it has its disadvantages. Its early seventeenth-century idiom is not that of the present day. Venerable as it is, modern people find it hard to understand. Further, its very familiarity to some of us can be a real barrier to understanding what it means. So what? Some people would like to relegate the AV to a museum of antiquities, but it would surely be a pity to do that. The language difficulty can be exaggerated; after all, Shakespeare's English belongs to the same period, and nobody suggests that he should be thrown out. Moreover, still looking at it purely from the literary point of view, readers themselves unversed in the AV would miss much of the allusiveness and quality of such masters of modern English as Kipling and John Buchan, who were so steeped in it that its rich, effective rhythms rolled from their tongues and pens as though they were their own.

For many of us, therefore, the solution may be to use

two versions, the AV and another. The makers of the
Revised Version of 1881 were concerned at once to
better the translation of the Authorized, and to preserve
its style. They did succeed in making the original meaning clearer, but their pseudo-seventeenth century language lacks the spontaneity of its model without elimin-
ating its archaic character. One may use either or both
of these authoritative versions, therefore, and still find
profit from a really modern one. There has been a spate
of these in recent years, and you can take your pick.
Moffatt's *A New Translation of the Bible*, published by
Hodder and Stoughton, is scholarly and readable; in
some of the prophetic passages it is brilliant. It has a
helpful introduction, and there is a small edition of the
New Testament alone, most handy for the pocket.
The Revised Standard Version, published by Nelson in
1952, and now available in a well-printed edition at
12s 6d, has made its way rapidly and is clearly meeting
a need. Mgr Ronald Knox's translation, published by
Burns and Oates and now authorized for use in the
Roman Catholic church, is fine reading for anyone, and
a vast improvement on the English versions previously
in vogue in that communion. Being made from the
Latin Vulgate, however, it is rather perplexing at times
to people whose acquaintance is with versions based
directly on the Hebrew and the Greek.

Moffatt, the RSV, and Knox are all complete translations of both Testaments, and the RSV has the Apoc-
rypha also, though in a separate volume. Apart from
the lack of this appendix to the Canon in the other two,

any one of these three versions may serve over the whole field of Scripture either to introduce us to Holy Writ *de novo*, or to break for us the crust of long and rather uncomprehending familiarity with the antique diction of AV and RV, and make the meaning come alive. Besides these, there is one outstanding translation of the New Testament only, and two of parts of it. The former is J. B. Phillips' *New Testament in Modern English*, published by Geoffrey Bles in 1958; in their original form the four parts were called *The Gospels in Modern English*, *Letters to Young Churches* (the Epistles), *The Young Church in Action* (Acts), and *The Book of Revelation*. Several at least of these may be had in a cheap edition. The two partial translations are *The Four Gospels*, by E. V. Rieu, in the Penguin series—if you get this, don't miss the introduction, which is excellent—and *The New Testament Letters Prefaced and Paraphrased*, by J. W. C. Wand, formerly Bishop of London. This last is published by the Oxford University Press.

So much for English versions. But the busy Christian should not be too sure that he must be content with these. Anyone who has learnt even one language other than his own at school with any degree of ease and pleasure has in him the ability to learn New Testament Greek. Many people who have never learnt another language could probably do it, if they have a feeling for words and a reasonable ear for music; and where the language faculty is present at all, its exercise can be the greatest refreshment after other work. There is a first-rate book available, specially written for students working by themselves—*The Elements of New Testament Greek*, by H. P. V. Nunn, published by the Cambridge University Press. It takes nothing for granted in the way of previous knowledge even of English grammar. There is a *Key to the Exercises* too, from which you can correct your work yourself. There are a few quite obvious mistakes in this, which will presumably be corrected in the next edition. In the meantime, it gives the student great satisfaction to spot them for himself. If you embark on Nunn, even if you only get an odd ten minutes here and there, you will soon be picking your way through the easier parts of the New Testament,[1] and finding them as fresh and vivid as if you had never set eyes on them before.

It is to be hoped that many will tackle New Testament Greek, for even a slight knowledge of it opens a new world in Bible reading. A few here and there, for all their busyness, may be moved to tackle Hebrew too. Here again there is a first-rate book available from which to teach yourself—A. B. Davidson's *Introductory Hebrew Grammar* (24th edition), published by T. and T. Clark, and *A Key to the Exercises* so sympathetic that the student feels that he is being personally taught. Hebrew looks alarming, but once you have mastered

---

[1] There are many editions of this. The most up-to-date one is that published by the British and Foreign Bible Society in 1958; or there is Souter's (2nd ed., 1947, published by OUP), but Westcott and Hort's or older editions of Nestle will serve just as well for ordinary use. There are also interleaved and interlinear translations, giving the translation with the text.

the script and got used to reading from right to left instead of left to right, you are really through the worst. It is a very simple language both in structure and in thought, extraordinarily just and regular in its principles, and the vocabulary of the Old Testament is small. I believe the Jews say that Hebrew is spoken in heaven. It is certainly a language of vision, most deeply rewarding. So learn it if you can.

There remains Latin. This is not the original language of any of the Bible, but the Vulgate version in use today goes back to ancient sources. Its Latin is—as its name implies—that of the common people; so if you learned the classical variety at school, you must prepare for shocks. All the same, it is illuminating to read and to compare with English versions, if not also with the originals.

After the question of versions of the Bible comes that of books about it. Some people are readier to read these than to read the Bible itself, but that is a mistake. It may be that some of us ought deliberately to fast from reading books like these at times, and force ourselves to read the Bible only. Certainly one of the most thought-provoking and penetrating books about the Gospels written in this century was the work of an itinerant missionary in Central Africa, a thousand miles from a theological library and driven by that fact to read and re-read his Greek Testament.[1] All the same, we need some help from books. What books are they to be?

[1] *John, Peter and the Fourth Gospel*, by G. W. Broomfield, SPCK, 1934.

There are many to choose from nowadays, on many levels. Some are books to possess and refer to again and again; others are books to borrow and read once, making a few notes. A general reference book, such as *Black's Bible Dictionary* by M. S. and J. L. Miller (A. and C. Black, 1954), or Dr Lowther Clarke's *Concise Commentary on the Bible* (SPCK, 1952), or *A Theological Word Book of the Bible*, or *The Teacher's Commentary* (both edited by Professor Alan Richardson and published by the SCM Press), is of course a treasure. After that, the parts of the Bible that people mostly need help with are the prophets and epistles, especially St Paul's. Here again the choice is wide; but as introductions G. Caiger's *Lives of the Prophets* (SPCK, 1949) and H. N. Bate, *A Guide to the Epistles of St Paul* (Longmans, 1926), take a lot of beating. With the prophets, here is the suggested method. Begin with Amos, because he came first in time. Read the Book of Amos in the Bible through, in one if not two versions, noticing for yourself what seem to be the divisions of the subject-matter. Then read Caiger's or a one-volume *Commentary* chapter on Amos, looking up the references given. With the epistles, take Galatians first and read it carefully, and then write down in your own words what situation it envisages and what you think St Paul is getting at. If this comes to precious little, never mind. At least it is your own, the fruit of your own thought, not someone else's. That done, read the relevant section in Bate or the *Commentary*, again with references; then read the whole epistle through again. You will be getting inside Galatians by that time; it will have come alive. And so on with the rest.

As to books for reading once, people are differently situated. Some have access to good county or other public libraries, which will get books on request. Others—it may be in the mission field—are miles from anywhere and mostly too poor to buy. A possibility in the latter case is for several people to form a book society. Four of them, let us say, or maybe more, or even only two, agree to buy one book a year about the Bible or about Christian doctrine, of which of course the Bible is the source, notifying each other of their choices so that no two get the same. Each buyer has first go at his own book, and then they circulate, each book returning to its owner in the end. That means that each not only gets the chance to read several books a year, and to discuss them with his mates, but is himself collecting a small library of worthwhile books that he can lend, or himself read again some day.[1]

These are, as I have emphasized, suggestions only. Some who read this doubtless already use a leaflet such as that issued by the Bible Reading Fellowship, which provides a scheme for daily reading, together with some notes about the passages prescribed. Those leaflets are put together with much prayer and thought, and can be very helpful. There is however a certain danger in their use. Having a passage set and thoughts provided on it

[1] The simplest scholarly commentaries available are *The Torch Bible Commentaries*, published by the SCM Press. The SCM Press announces a new series, *The Layman's Bible Commentaries*, for those without any previous knowledge.

can make me lazy about thinking and praying for my-self, and so may make me miss some other thing the Holy Spirit wants to say to me. It may in fact lead me to hide my single talent in the earth, instead of trading with it; and that is not the way to treat the gift of God. In any case, most of us need to ring the changes in our method of Bible reading. Sometimes we may be guided to read a few verses and then stop and think. At others we shall be led, perhaps, to read a chapter, or several chapters, or even a whole gospel or epistle, straight on end, it may be even at a sitting, if we can get the time. Again, times come when a single word or theme will dance us from text to text all over the Bible. And at yet others a single word or verse will hold us, it may be for days.

No one can legislate for you exactly what you ought to do. As has been said, that is between you and the Holy Spirit, part of his intimation to you of your secret and peculiar 'new name'. But read the Bible you must, in one way or another; and feed on it you must, in your heart by faith with thanksgiving, for it is the very Word of life. And however busy you are, you *will* make time for it, provided that you are convinced it is a duty, part of the worship that you owe to God.

12

WORSHIP ALL THE TIME:
1. Ways and Means

WE HAVE SEEN that, according to the Bible, the life of
man consists in right relationship with God. His duty,
the worship that he, the creature, owes to his Creator,
is to love him back with all his heart, and soul, and
mind, and strength. That much is general, and true of
every man. The case of Christians is particular. Owing
to their sacramental incorporation into the act of God
in Christ, they are *in* Jesus Christ, and he is in them.
They are descendants of the old and fallen Adam, yet
they are also members of the New. As St Paul puts it,
they live, and yet not they, but Christ that liveth in
them,[1] Christ the perfect Man, who worships perfectly.
This adorable mystery is absolutely fundamental. It is—
or ought to be—the wellspring of all we do, the deter-
mining, enabling factor in every action and activity.

That is the Christian life, and what a life it is! We
have already thought a bit about some of the aspects
and departments of it. We have considered the public,
corporate worship which we call 'going to church', in
its two parts, the Holy Eucharist and the Choir Office.
We have thought also about our so-called 'private'

[1] See Gal. 2.20.

prayer, which nonetheless is still prayer in and with the Church, Christ's Body; here in particular we discussed how best to use set times of prayer, and went on to examine at what may have seemed great length to some the vital matter of our Bible reading. But still we have not done. St Paul says, 'Pray *without ceasing*.'[1] No, he is not—as you might think—addressing cloistered monks and nuns with nothing else to do but say their prayers; there were not any in AD 51, and anyhow, though few believe it, such people really do a lot of work. He is addressing new converts recently baptized, a tiny handful of believers living in a pagan world. He is in fact addressing busy Christians like ourselves.

And he is not inventing something new to lay on Christian shoulders. He is simply giving them our Lord's own recipe for holiness. 'Pray without ceasing' is only the first part of it. The whole injunction reads:

'Pray without ceasing,
    in everything give thanks;
    for this is the will of Jesus Christ concerning you.'

'The will of Jesus Christ concerning YOU,' of Jesus Christ who said—and says—to his disciples, 'Be ye therefore perfect, as your Father in heaven is perfect.'[2] 'Perfect' does not mean merely not having any sin. It means complete, integrated, and this in the case of man the creature means fulfilling the purpose for which he was created, obeying the Creator. Further, the Creator is the creature's pattern of perfection, because the creature is

[1] I Thess. 5.17.   [2] Matt. 5.48.

made in the Creator's image. The perfecting of man consists in the development in him to the full extent of his capacity of his germinal likeness to Almighty God. This is a 'counsel of perfection' with a vengeance. But it is addressed to ALL the followers of Jesus Christ. So we must face it, staggering though it is, and try to think out how it may be carried out.

The busy Christian's daily life, seen as a sequence of events in time, is rather like a necklace of assorted beads. In each day's string there are, we hope, three or at least two periods of time directly occupied by private prayer; on certain days at least there are rather longer periods of corporate prayer in church. All the rest of the twenty-four hours goes in eating, sleeping—or anyhow in trying to sleep, working in one way or another, recreation, travelling, talking to people, and so forth. Almost any one of these occupations probably gets longer stretches of time and a generally larger share of it than we devote to prayer. In terms of the necklace, these are large, fat beads of different colours, and there are many of them; whereas the golden beads of prayer are relatively small, and few and far between. In fact, anybody looking at the necklace might not notice that they were there at all. A necklace, however, implies a connecting thread of some sort, on which all the beads are strung. In any life there is, by the fact of its being a life, the connecting thread of the individual's continued physical existence; it is the same person who does all the things. But in the Christian's case there is a second one. There is the thread of grace, of Christ's life in his member. We have seen that, when the Christian prays, because he prays in Christ, it is in a true sense also Christ who prays in him. But you cannot have him only pray in you. He is not given to indwell you only for those brief times. When you rise from your knees, he does not leave you, returning only when you kneel again. He stays with you, that he may work and sleep and eat and think and talk and recreate in you. If you keep him out of these activities, you will be forcing him to say with the psalmist, 'I am so fast in prison that I cannot get forth,'[1] and that is not the way to treat Almighty God.

This is not fancy teaching. It is plain, basic Christianity. In the prologue to the Acts of the Apostles the author refers to the Gospels as the record of 'all that Jesus *began* both to do and teach' while he was on earth.[2] The implication is that the acts of the apostles, which he is now going to recount, are the continued acts of Jesus, carried on through them. In the days of his flesh our Lord prayed without ceasing, in that whatever he did, he did it to God's glory, because God wanted it and as he wanted it;[3] this made his every act, however trivial, an expression of his love and so an act of worship, of giving God his due. He gave thanks in everything because, believing in God's utter love for him and for mankind and all creation, he took whatever came as from his hand; and that thanksgiving culminated 'in the same night in which he was betrayed'. So he redeemed the world. Now—when we let him—he

---

[1] Ps. 88.8.   [2] Acts 1.1 f.   [3] See Heb. 10.5-7.

carries on his saving work through us and in us. That is
his method, and he has no other, till he comes again. As
he acted and taught for three and thirty years in the
body that he took of Mary, using his hands and feet and
lips and eyes and ears and every part of him as need
required to do the work his Father had given him to do,
so since the Day of Pentecost he has been continuing
that saving work—that work that paradoxically he had
accomplished once for all on Calvary—through his
mystical Body the Church as a whole, and through her
individual members severally. Those include you. And
me. That is the calling wherewith you and I are called,
to *serve* our Lord and Saviour as a man's limbs obey his
mind and will. We are called to be his fellow-workers,[1]
to let him carry on and carry out his saving, recreating
work both in and through us, to *help* him in his work.
That is terrific, shattering; but it is true. Just that is
what it means to be a Christian, nothing less. But how
on earth—quite literally how on earth—are we to
answer this astounding call?

First and last, response to the call of God is a matter
of will, because it is a matter of love, and there can be
no love without the will to love. It is really rather com-
forting that this is so, for our will is the one thing
always in our own power. You can never altogether
help your feelings in this world, and our Lord's own
anguish on Gethsemane[2] shows that even he, the
perfect Man, could not help his. Your circumstances
also may be quite beyond your power to change;

---

[1] See II Cor. 6.1.   [2] Mark 14.32 ff. and parallels.

only your will is always in your power, infirm though it may be.

Now earlier in this chapter we compared the Christian's daily life to a necklace of assorted beads strung not on one thread only, but on two. The second thread, you will remember, is the thread of supernatural, enabling grace, the life of Christ in you. That thread in a manner of speaking carries a current. If that current is allowed to run freely and uninterruptedly, it will light up all the beads as it goes through, even the commonest and dullest of them, and will make them uniformly beautiful. This is the idea behind the song that some of you may know, that is called *The Glow Within*:

> 'Oh, you gotta getta glory
> In the work you do,
> A Hallelujah chorus
> In the heart of you!
>
> 'Paint, or tell a story,
> Sing, or shovel coal,
> But you gotta get a glory,
> Or the work lacks soul.'[1]

It rests with you—and it is up to you—to let that blessed, glory-making current run, by uniting your will always and in everything with the will of Christ for you. Just in so far as you do that, you will be praying without ceasing and giving thanks in everything.

No one becomes perfect all at once, and the Christian needs a lot of patience with himself. As Bishop Gore

[1] I suppose that this is a negro spiritual, but the card on which I found the words named neither author nor publisher.

used to say, however, 'There is no failure except in ceasing to try.' So let us think how we can try, and go on trying, to rise up to God's call.

The starting-point for each new day is obviously morning prayer. With that first golden bead, you set your will, as you might set a compass or wind up your watch, to love God back throughout the coming day, whatever it may bring. You might do worse than use George Herbert's hymn:

> 'Teach me, my God and King,
> In all things thee to see;
> And what I do in anything
> To do it as for thee.'

You may well use also the prayer of St Ignatius Loyola:

> 'O beloved Word of God, teach me to be generous,
> Teach me to serve thee as thou deservest,
> To give, and not to count the cost,
> To fight, and not to heed the wounds,
> To toil, and not to seek for rest,
> To labour, and to ask for no reward
> Save that of knowing that I do thy will.'

So you start the day quite simply aiming at perfection. Your will is united to God's, so the current is running. The thing is to keep it so.

Speaking generally, the rest of a person's daily occupations, widely varied though these are in different cases, fall into two groups. Some of them require one's whole attention. Some do not. Those that do require it must have it. As William Temple said, 'If I am to serve God perfectly, I must sometimes forget him.' For many of us, there are long hours in the day when we just cannot do our work and think of God at the same time. But this should worry no one. Your conscious mind has to forget him in these occupations, for it cannot give itself entirely to more than one thing at a time. But the intention to do everything for God persists in your subconscious, and if you are doing your work as well as you possibly can, then the current is still running and your work is prayer. All the same, since we are what we are, our Godward intention needs to be often reinforced. That of course is where set times of prayer come in, to stoke the fires of love. But we do not have to wait for those. Even in the very thick of these engrossing occupations, the loving heart will snatch a second here and there to look at God, to catch his eye for orders, so to speak, and send up a brief prayer for help and blessing. And then there are the in-between-times of the day, and the occupations that do not take one's whole attention. What can we do with those?

The answer is, two things. First, we can make them acts and times of worship, just as we make the other, more engrossing occupations worship, by the simple fact of our continued and avowed intention to do them for the Lord. If washing-up, for instance, is the next thing to be done, then, if I do it willingly and well *because* it is the next thing to be done according to God's ordering of my day, then my washing-up, offered in that spirit, is an act of worship, and that prosaic bead becomes a jewel in his sight. The same applies to all the commonplace and humdrum things of daily life, as much as to the great demands. Some people seem afraid to admit this. They have an uneasy notion that it is somehow insulting to Almighty God to offer him such humble things. But to think thus is to minimise the wonder of the Incarnation. The Son of God not only took our flesh; he lived in it, and to God's glory without any show did in it all the ordinary things about the place that all men do, and no extraordinary ones at all, until almost the end. If he is to extend his Incarnation in us, he must be allowed to do these ordinary things in us, as well as the big ones that sometimes come. The opportunities of little things, moreover, are not precious only in themselves. They are practice exercises in the essential art of taking what comes. If you baulk at all the little low jumps every day, how can you hope to clear the rope when suddenly one day it is put high?

> 'Whatever thy hand findeth to do,
>   do it with thy might;
>   that God in all things may be glorified.'[1]

Secondly, these in-between-times and occupations that do not take one's whole attention are golden opportunities for direct prayer. If you take them as such, they will help very greatly to reinforce your general intention to serve God at intervals more frequent than those provided by set times of prayer. They will help tremendously to keep the current running between the set times and the times of all-out work.

You cannot pray in quite the same way in these times

[1] Eccles. 9.10, plus the response to it at Prayers at the Alice Ottley School, Worcester.

as in the set ones; for one thing, they do not generally admit the bodily concomitants of prayer. But the set times can to a considerable extent provide the material for the in-betweens. In the set times you store your memory. You say a psalm, a hymn, a collect, or some other prayer, or you read a Bible passage till you know it by heart. Then in the bus on the way to work, or in your own car as you drive along, or in the queue at the grocer's, or when you are waiting in outpatients' at the hospital, or weeding the garden, or peeling the potatoes, or minding a machine, or whatever the thing may be, you go to the cupboard, so to speak, and take out a bone to suck, something to say, and say again, and ponder on.

'The Lord is my Shepherd: therefore can I lack nothing.'

'Come, Holy Ghost, our souls inspire,
And lighten with celestial fire . . .'

'Graft in our hearts the love of thy name;
increase in us true religion . . .'

'O beloved Word of God, teach me to be generous . . .'

'The fruit of the Spirit is love, joy, peace . . .'[1]

Those are just specimens. In some of the in-between times you can use a book. Some people can fit in their Bible reading, or at least some of it, on their daily ride to work. A few might even learn to read their Greek New Testament that way. But that does not exhaust the uses of these times. They are splendid, never-ceasing opportunities for intercession. Wherever you go, you

[1] Ps. 23; the *Veni Creator*; Collect for the Seventh Sunday after Trinity; Prayer of St. Ignatius (cited on p. 93); Gal. 5.22 ff.

see people, and you hear of people. They all belong to God. He made and loves every one of them. Christ died for every one of them, and every one of them is capable of God and made for God; though many are not using that capacity, and so just are not really living a *human* life at all. Well, look at every person that you see like that, and pray for them. *Want* him or her for God, both for God's sake who loves them so, and theirs, whose need of him is so entire. Pray in the same way for the people of whom you read in the papers, the people whose names you see on the posters and outside cinemas and theatres, the people whose voices you hear on the wireless, whose faces you see on TV, the people inside all the buildings that you see. Just pray 'Bless, bless, bless . . .' They are all God's whether they know it or not. He created them all for himself, and all their hearts are restless till they rest in him.

Another way of interceding in the in-between and half-and-half times is on what may be called the circle system. Circles have centres. In a true sense we are self-centred beings because each person's consciousness of everything outside himself is *ipso facto* centred in himself. From this it follows that, in his relationships with other people and indeed the whole created order, the individual is the centre of a whole lot of circles, and for all within those circles the Christian ought to pray. First for most of us, there is the circle of one's family. Then there is the circle with whom our lot is thrown at work, and there may well be others, societies, trade unions, and so forth, in individual cases. In any case there is probably a further circle of one's friends, apart from relatives and those with whom we work. There is also the circle of one's immediate co-religionists and fellow-countrymen; an Anglican, for instance, will want to pray for the whole Church of England and the whole people of Britain, his own parish, diocese, and place of residence especially; and with and beyond these he will look out on to the wider circles of the whole Anglican communion and the British Commonwealth. But he will not stop there. He will look round next on Christendom entire and the whole human race at present upon earth; and, ranging further yet, his thought will reach to that far vaster portion of humanity beyond the veil, which with ourselves awaits the Final Consummation.[1] Lastly, he will remember that, as a human being, he is a part also of the whole creation, and will lay that also, earth, vegetation, animals, sun, moon, and stars, before his Father's feet, praying that his will for all of it may be fulfilled.

It is a good thing to make up your own list of circles on these lines, because it fosters your sense of belonging and of responsibility to each; and, once you have made it, you can run through it in your head at almost any time, simply remembering the fact of each in turn, and bringing it to God.

Again, you can do a particular piece of work with intention for some special person or cause or need. You can make an offering of it to God, doing it the very best you can, and asking him to accept it for that cause or

---

[1] See Heb. 11.40.

person. Or, in the case especially of manual occupations, like gardening or handicrafts, that often leave a part of the attention free, one can most blessedly 'be still and know',[1] letting the love of God fall on one's soul like rain on thirsty ground, rejoicing in the simple fact of being loved by him.

Set times, work times, in-between and half-and-half times, all can be prayer, and all can be thanksgiving. There remains only sleep.

Sleep is a mystery. Each day of our life is a type and microcosm of the whole, having in it all the elements that go to make the whole; and the sleep of each night symbolizes death. It is a holy thing and a most precious gift of God. When he lies down to sleep, the Christian should commit himself to God, body and soul. God will then go on working in him while he sleeps, the current will still run. He should ask God for sleep, and thank for it on waking; he should not take it for granted, as though he had a right to it, and if it is withheld, he must be patient. If he is awake in the night, there is another chance for prayer. St Bernard thought those night times were the best times of all.

It really is possible by the grace of God to pray without ceasing and to give thanks in all things, even in the busiest life. Some people manage it; and just how lovely they are to live with has to be experienced to be believed. But it is not easy, and one does not learn it in a day. In the next chapter, therefore, we will consider the chief hindrances to this unceasing prayer.

[1] Ps. 46.10.

13

WORSHIP ALL THE TIME:
II. Hindrances

WORSHIP, AS WE WELL KNOW, means giving God his due, and what is due from us to God is love. So we fail in worship just so often as we fail in love. Ultimately all our sins and failures great and small stem from that one root; and they all hinder the unceasing worship to which we are called. All of them, moreover, are offences against God himself. Ultimately again, each one of us if he is honest must say of every sin he does, 'Against Thee only have I sinned.[1] But while some of our sins are done directly against him, others are done against him in some creature that belongs to him. So it is convenient to discuss sins under these two heads.

The law of love under the Old Covenant was first

'Thou shalt love the Lord thy God with all thy heart, and with all thy soul, and with all thy mind, and with all thy strength,'[2]

and then

'Thou shalt love thy neighbour as thyself.'[3]

Of those twin commandments our Lord said that there

[1] Ps. 51.4.   [2] Deut. 6.5.   [3] Lev. 19.8.

was none greater, and that upon them hung the whole of the law and the prophets.[1] Of the law and the prophets, he also said that he had come not to destroy but to fulfil them.[2] The word 'fulfil' has two senses; its use here covers both. Our Lord 'fulfilled' this law of love, in that, as Man, he kept it perfectly in both its parts; and it was by that perfect keeping even unto death that he revoked the Fall and, as the *Te Deum* puts it, opened the kingdom of heaven to all believers. He 'fulfilled' it in the other sense, in that he also sublimated it, lifted it higher, demonstrated it, and made it far more rich and also more demanding. On the night before he died, he said to his disciples in the upper room,

> 'A new commandment I give unto you, that ye love one another; *even as I have loved you*, that ye love one another.'[3]

It is from this 'new commandment', given in close association with and pointed by the institution of the Eucharist, and spoken only to the inner circle of his friends, that Maundy Thursday, the Thursday of the Maundy or Command, derives its name. Two days before, however, he had given another lesson about love of general application. In the parable (so-called) of the sheep and the goats he had revealed the single principle by which mankind in general is to be judged by him, as Son of Man. Each man's eternal destiny depends on his behaviour to his fellow-men, *because* what any one man does to any other, whether of good or evil, of un-

[1] Mark 12.31; Matt. 22.40.   [2] Matt. 5.17.   [3] John 13.34.

love or of love, is in fact done to him, the all-inclusive Man.[1]

So we have as it were a trinity of laws of love to keep. We have the law of love for God with our whole being. We have the general law of loving action in respect of all our fellow-men. We have also the special law of love for those who, like ourselves, are friends of our dear Lord. Where do we mostly fail in each of these?

We fail in love directly Godward every time we fail to take what comes.

> 'If on our daily course our mind
> Be set to hallow all we find,
> New treasures still, of countless price,
> God will provide for sacrifice.
>
> 'The trivial round, the common task,
> Will furnish all we need to ask,
> Room to deny ourselves, a road
> To bring us daily nearer God.'[2]

That could not be truer. The point is that all the things that come to you, whether they be pleasant or unpleasant as far as tastes and feelings go, are in themselves of neutral quality. They are made to be good or bad, blessings or curses for *you*, *by* you, simply, by the way in which you take them.

In respect of the pleasant things, the danger is of taking them for granted, of forgetting that they are the gifts of God, given not once for all and in the lump, but singly, graciously, continually, in every case his per-

[1] Matt. 25.31 ff.   [2] Part of John Keble's hymn, 'New every morning is the love'.

sonal gift, whatever the created agency through which they come. This is a matter in which Christians can learn a lot from Jews. We put a lot of emphasis on asking God for things. With the Jews, as the psalms bear witness, praise and thanksgiving for what he has already done and given always take first place. The synagogue liturgy has the same character today; God is 'blessed' in the daily services for light and darkness, for bringing on the twilight, for the stars, for making Israel his People and for giving them the law, for bread and wine, for sustaining the living and quickening the dead and keeping faith with them, and many other things. Further, blessings are prescribed for private use on such occasions as tasting any fruit for the first time that season, receiving tidings whether good or bad, putting on new clothes, and seeing the new moon.[1] We ought to give God thanks for things like this, and many more. As St Paul says, he gives us 'richly all things to enjoy'.[2] We should enjoy them, it is churlish to do otherwise. To quote the Jews again, they have a saying that for every legitimate pleasure that a man refuses to enjoy in this world, he will be docked of one in the next. That is quite an idea. We certainly need to develop our power of enjoyment in this life, if we look to enjoy the next; and a sensitive appreciation of its smaller things is an authentic mark of the true Christian and a wonderful help in making the wheels go round. Some pious

[1] See Singer, *The Authorised Daily Prayer Book of the United Hebrew Congregations of the British Empire*, 7th ed., Eyre and Spottiswoode, 1904. [2] I Tim. 6.17.

people have a notion that it is 'worldly' to enjoy things like their food, but that is nonsense. What *is* worldly, as distinct from Christian, is not to be grateful for it, or to complain when it is bad or lacking. Which brings us to the second sort of things that come, those that we find repugnant.

With some of these, the trouble is that we get taken by surprise. We set our intention in the morning to 'hallow all we find' by taking it in love as from God's loving hand; and then things happen suddenly to vex us, and we jib. We feel it an affront that things should happen so to us, and fall into self-pity. Instead of giving thanks to God for the thing we mislike, in effect we throw it back at him and say, 'Take it away!'.

In one sense, failure of this sort is fundamental, and cannot be too seriously taken. However small the contradiction and however mild the reaction of rejection, refusal of it is a refusal of the cross; it is a taking back what we have given to God and a turning back from the plough, and it negates both the homage of our hands put between his in prayer and the stretching of them open to receive the host and chalice, with all that fellowship with Christ entails. It is a radical sin—*the* radical sin, and it must be treated at the root. Self-pity must be frankly recognized for what it is—just plain disloyalty to God and, as such, deadly poison to the soul.

Yet in another sense these failures can be allowed to weigh too heavily. If I, for instance, show impatience at an interruption, undoubtedly I sin. But the devil's concern in the affair is not so much to lead me into that

initial expression of annoyance as to make me annoyed
with myself for being annoyed, and so to reduce me to
an emotional mess, resulting really from hurt pride, in
which I shall neither work nor pray. Yet that initial
failure on such occasions is really a small matter in
itself. It is a spontaneous reaction, not deliberate. It
shows you that your will is weak as yet; if it were not,
it would be less susceptible to such surprise attacks. All
the same, the share of your will in it thus far is negative, rather than positive; you did not want nor did you
mean to do it. So if at this point, instead of staying
down and getting crosser, you get up at once and turn
to God in penitence for your involuntary stumble, the
situation is saved. The contradiction, which God
allowed even if the devil did contrive it, has served his
purpose, not the Enemy's. Because you have refused to
be discouraged by your fall, that connecting, sanctify-
ing, glory-giving current, which we have thought of as
running through our daily life, making worship out of
all we do, is running again; it may be all the stronger
for its momentary check. By turning the humiliation of
your failure into humility, you have made the evil
minister to its own overthrow; for now your will is
strengthened to meet the next attack. 'Sold again,
Satan!', as the small child said on recognizing and re-
sisting a temptation. And Bishop Gore would say that
there had been no failure, for you have not ceased to try.

If on the other hand you justify it to yourself, or—
which is just as deadly—fall into depression over it,
forgetting that it is against God only that you have

offended, your will is weakened, and the foe at his next onslaught finds you an easy prey.

For many people, the day is full of such attacks, but not all take us by surprise. Some of them we know that we shall have to meet. Most of us have bugbears somewhere in our lives, things that we loathe and naturally wish away. It may be some physical handicap; we must deal with those in the next chapter. Or it may be some repugnant thing that you have frequently to do, or some other circumstance in life that you are up against continually. These things constitute both a deadly peril and a life-giving opportunity. If they are not bravely faced and dealt with Christianly, they cause what may be called thrombosis of the soul, stopping the circulation. There is one way and one only to disperse the clot; that is to make one's will accept the hateful thing and positively give God thanks for it. Thanking him does not by any means preclude your asking him to take the thing away, if it be possible; even our Lord did that.[1] But it does mean that you set your will to trust his love, to see him in the thing you so dislike, to see him looking through the lattice of it at you, like the Bridegroom in the Song of Songs, calling through it to you, his beloved, to rise up and come away with him.[2]

We come now to the two laws of love towards our neighbour, the general and the particular. The elder law

[1] Mark 14.36. [2] Song of Songs 2.9. Origen, who was almost the first of the Fathers to interpret the song mystically, read 'nets' for 'lattices', and equated them with the 'snares of the fowler', i.e., the temptations of the devil. It is *through* these that the Lord looks at us.

had the one commandment only, 'Thou shalt love thy neighbour *as thyself.*' This implies that there is a right self-love, a sense in which we *ought* to love ourselves, and err if we do not. The right self-love loves self because God does, and for no other reason. It wants what God wants for itself, and nothing else. This is no more than common sense. How shall we *not* love the self that God has made, that he so loves, and for which our dear Lord took flesh, and died, and rose again? Pious writers sometimes speak of 'hatred of self' as the necessary concomitant of love for God, and the mark of the saint; but that is wrong. We have to hate our *sins*, for they are blemishes on God's beloved, but most emphatically we are NOT to hate ourselves.

For the same reason, we are required to hate other people's sins, but love themselves. It is easy to say that, and to point the distinction in words, but very difficult to do it. You cannot separate a person from his faults that perhaps hit you in the eye, as maybe yours do him. How then is it possible to hate the one, and yet to love the other?

The answer comes out of that description of what will happen on the Day of Judgement, to which we referred just now. The Incarnate Son of God has so identified himself with Man that he includes all men. In the dear old evangelical phrase, we have therefore to 'see the Lord' in them. Sometimes this is quite easy, and you can't help doing it. He has a way of peeping out from most imperfect people on occasion, even from those who barely know his name, and in the truly holy and humble of heart he is never far to seek. But at other times and with many people he is so wholly hidden that to see him in them, and to act accordingly, calls for heroic faith. But the effort of faith must be made, for of all the hindrances to worship in our lives, there is none greater than failure in charity towards our neighbour.

Sometimes this comes from sheer lack of thought and self-absorption. We are so taken up with our own affairs and the immediate circle of people with whom we have to do, that we just have no eyes—or heart—for anyone outside it. A year or two ago there was a letter —in the *Church Times*, I think—from an ex-prisoner. He had learnt religion while serving his sentence, and after his release attended a certain village church twice every Sunday for six weeks. In the course of that time, no other worshipper took any notice of him whatsoever. It was not because he was a gaol-bird, for he was unknown in the place. It was just that the congregation was a closed shop, and its members were not interested in anyone outside. Like Dives, they simply did not see the beggar at their gate, so his sores went untended.[1]

Many who read this will say, 'That could not happen in *our* church,' and we may well thank God that that is so. But such limitation of charity is extremely common, and in many spheres. How many people do *you* see, every day it may be, of whom you know nothing and care less? Those girls in Woolworth's, for instance, on their feet all day in that exhausted atmosphere; yet in them Christ is daily offering himself to you for love. Are

[1] See Luke 16.19 ff.

you responding? Look out for Lazarus, Christian, and serve him while you can.

The sort of universal intercession which we advocated in the last chapter is a good antidote to this sort of thoughtlessness and negative indifference to other people's needs. But by no means all our failures in charity are of that kind. Many of them come from positive antipathies, and take an active, rather than a passive form. They usually start with something very small. You take offence at something someone does or says. Much oftener than not, there is an element of misunderstanding in it, but you are not generous enough to think of or allow for that; you assume the worst and treat it as a fact. In fact, you have a grudge. Thereafter you regard that person with a jaundiced eye, which means that you subconsciously at least expect them to offend in the same sort of way again. Meanwhile the other person is probably feeling in much the same way about you. So it goes on. And where in all this is the love of God and of one's neighbour?

In the Anglican liturgy, intending communicants are expressly required to be in love and charity with all their neighbours. That this is a *sine qua non* of worthy reception is obvious. Nevertheless the lives of many otherwise religious people are spoilt by misrelationships like these. We are far too easy-going with ourselves about such things. We think they do not matter very much, and can't be helped, and anyhow the other person is the most to blame, and we have done our best. But they do matter. They matter utterly, in any case;

and when they are between Christians, whose duty it is to love each other *as their Lord loves them*, they are quite damnable and devastating in the harm they do, both to the individuals concerned and to the Church, as well as to outsiders who are scandalized. If we want to worship all the time, as we are called to do, and if we do not want to suffer from thrombosis of the soul, we *must* deal with them and correct them, at whatever cost. Here are a few practical suggestions as to how this may be done.

First and foremost and all the time, let us frankly recognize that, if those blessed twins, the senses of humour and proportion, were always in full working order as they should be in a Christian life, such deplorable situations as we are envisaging simply would not arise. Those senses are intrinsic elements in love, and integral to a full human life. Let us thank God for them, and make full use of them. Where such situations do exist, the following points may be observed.

First, as a necessary safeguard, one should bind oneself by a solemn promise made to God in prayer never to speak of anyone's shortcomings to a third person without real necessity—never, that is, to do so merely to relieve one's feelings and get sympathy. Failure to keep this promise must be confessed as sin.

Second, one must be very brave and honest in searching one's own heart. You can be pretty sure that pride comes into your unfortunate reactions to that person, and there may be jealousy as well. Out with it, then. Admit it and condemn it. If there has been open friction between you and the other, and words have passed between you that are matter for regret, then apologize without delay for your share in the fault. *Someone* has got to begin; it had better be you.

Thirdly, one must take every chance that offers of showing friendly to the person whom one has got across. This approach, however, must be humble, not *de haut en bas*. Nothing is more alienating to an already exacerbated B than self-conscious magnanimity on the part of A. One should be at least as genuinely ready to put oneself in the other's debt for help and kindness, as to put him in one's own. In some cases this may involve turning a blind eye and a deaf ear to quite a lot for quite a time; but few people's defences can stand up indefinitely to the assault of genuine, effective[1] love, which is what these tactics are, and many ultimately staunch and lifelong friends have been made and won in this way. Moreover, truly Christian meekness is not weakness; it is strength, for it requires tremendous self-control. You put up with a lot, perhaps, and some may say that you are letting the other person wipe his boots on you, and showing lack of spirit. Of course some characters do let themselves be dominated and browbeaten by others of a more aggressive temperament; but that is quite a different thing, and good for neither party. The generous forbearance that we are advocating here is good for both of you. It is good for A to practise active love to B, and try 'to see the Lord' in him, regardless of his

[1] I.e., effective as distinct from affective; love that acts, not love that feels.

feelings; and it is good for B to have the best believed of him. Further, only the truly humble person in the part of A, the one who is normally forbearing almost to a fault, will have the grace and power on occasion to stand up to B and—as the modern idiom has it—show him where he gets off. Such rare but unequivocal rebuke, given in gentleness and selflessly and prompted by the Spirit, will take effect where a score of heated tellings-off only make matters worse. But no one can hope to act A's part like that, unless he is prepared to take occasional rebuke himself.

Lastly, this line of action is a fulfilment of the 'new commandment'. To put it mildly, our Lord puts up with a great deal from us. He helps us; yet in his great humility he seeks our help. He fully knows the worst of us, yet he believes the best. He loves us whole. He loves us redemptively, constructively, creatively. In fact, his love is what St Paul describes:

'Love is patient and kind;
  love is not jealous or boastful;
  it is not arrogant or rude.
Love does not insist on its own way;
  it is not irritable or resentful;
  it does not rejoice at wrong, but rejoices in the right.
Love bears all things,
  believes all things
  endures all things,
  hopes all things.
Love never ends.'[1]

That love he requires from us towards each other.

[1] I Cor. 13.4-7, *Moffatt's translation* RSV.

14

'THIS VILE BODY'

THE EXPRESSION 'this vile body' comes to us from St Paul, or rather from the Authorized Version of St Paul.[1] In common speech, however, it is frequently used by people ignorant of its context, if not also of its authorship, in much the same way as the expression 'What a life!' The circumstances in which it is used, and the tone in which the words are said, suggest in either case that things are pretty poor and we should like them better.

Things to that effect about the body are so often said. We modern people live at a great pace in a distracted world, and our bodies feel the strain. We tend in consequence to become unbalanced about our bodily health; this is in fact a disease-minded age. Nevertheless, most of us would agree that the body should be kept in its place; but to do that you must first be clear what its place is. This knowledge is of supreme importance for the Christian, for many of his spiritual problems are bound up with it. So in this chapter we will think about the doctrine of the body according to the Christian faith.

[1] Phil. 3.21.

The chief exponent of this doctrine of the body is St Paul, and really to study his teaching would take up a whole book. Here, at the end of this one, we can only summarize, and leave the reader to pursue the matter for himself.

St Paul says that our Lord Jesus Christ is the saviour of the body (Eph. 5.25), having suffered for it in his own (Col. 1.22; cf. Heb. 10.10); and that the body is *for* the Lord, and the Lord *for* the body.

He speaks of the body under three different figures. In regard to its relation Godward, he calls it the temple of the Holy Ghost (I Cor. 6.29).

Of its relation to the man himself, he uses an expression that is best translated 'this earthly tent of ours' (II Cor. 5.1; cf. II Peter 1.13 f.).

Lastly, with reference to its future, he compares it to a seed, such as a grain of wheat (I Cor. 15.35 ff.).

Temple, tent, seed. Let us take these in turn.

St Paul was a Jew born. For him, 'the temple' was the temple at Jerusalem, that holy 'palace of God', as it is called in Hebrew, of which the prophet quoted by our Lord said that it should be called the house of prayer.[1] *As such, it was the place of sacrifice.*

If we remember that, many other of St Paul's scattered teachings about the body fall into line with this statement that it is the temple of the Holy Ghost. There is for instance that passage where he speaks of himself and his fellow-Christians at Corinth as 'always bearing about in the body the dying of the Lord Jesus, that the

[1] Isa. 56.7, cited in Mark 11.17 and parallels.

life also of Jesus might be manifested in their body
(II Cor. 4.10). There is that in which he urges the Christians of Rome to present their bodies a living sacrifice,
holy, acceptable unto God, because that is their 'reasonable service' (Rom. 12.1). You have to go to the Greek
to get the force of that last phrase. 'Reasonable' means
elsewhere either 'rational', or 'metaphorical' as op-
posed to 'literal'. Both meanings are included here.
For the self-oblation required of the Christian in this
present life is rational, in that it must be made deliberately, with full intent and conscious will; it is however metaphorical in that it is a *living* sacrifice—i.e.,
the victim's life does not have to be released from the
body in order to be sacrificed.[1] The sacrifice consists
in living in the body, in union with the sacrifice of
Christ.

Again, there is the passage where he speaks of himself
as filling up the things that remain over of the sufferings
of Christ (Col. 1.24). A tremendous paradox which we
have met before confronts us here. The sufferings of
Christ were once for all and all-sufficient; no one was
ever more sure of that than was St Paul. Nevertheless,
the perfection of the Lord's oblation in the body that
he took of Mary has to be extended and reproduced in
his Body the Church, both as a whole and in its individual members. That is how the New Man is to become
eventually coextensive with the Old. That—and that

[1] I.e., you do not have to die a martyr's death to make
your life a sacrifice. Nevertheless, the Christian ought to regard
his death, however it occurs, as the crowning act of penance
and of sacrifice.

only—is the way redemption works. That is why St Paul wrote to his most disappointing and backsliding converts, 'I travail in birth again, till Christ be formed in you' (Gal. 4.19). That was why he himself eventually rejoiced even in his most humiliating physical infirmity, because God had convinced him that it is precisely through such weakness that power[1] is perfected (II Cor. 12.7-9).

Thus to form Christ the Victim in the Christian and thus to perfect power in weakness is the function of the Holy Ghost. In each of his temples he broods, to that intent. And all this happens while a man is still in the body, not in spite of the body, but by means of it.

A temple is a solid, permanent affair, and always in one spot. A tent, by contrast, is a frail and flimsy, not too comfortable dwelling-place, a 'house' only of sorts. A man bound for a destination where he expects to spend the rest of his life may use a tent while he is on his journey to that place; but, when he gets there, he will scrap the tent and move into a proper house, where he can stay. That is the idea in St Paul's mind in the first part of II Cor. 5. The point that he is driving home is that this body that a man now has is not his spirit's permanent abode. It is its house only for here and now, till death or till the Second Coming, as the case may be (I Thess. 4.15-17).

Then what?

---

[1] All our versions have 'My power', but there is no 'My' in the original.

That is a double question. Then what, at death? Then what, at the Last Day?

St Paul's interest is in the second question. He, who himself had seen the risen Lord in glory, is so taken up with looking forward to his own resurrection and that of all mankind at Christ's Return, that he passes over the intermediate state of those who die before that Day. To die will be gain, for it will be 'to be with Christ, which is far better'.[1] The dead 'sleep in Jesus'.[2] That is enough for him.

No positive revelation other than the above has been vouchsafed to us about that intermediate stage of human life, so nothing is of faith concerning it. It is permissible to think that the human spirit is never completely disembodied, never entirely without a 'house'. St Paul's words in II Cor. 5.4, about our being not un-clothed, but clothed upon after we leave this body, might refer to an interim body, as well as to the final one. St Augustine moreover says quite plainly in one of his books that neither soul *nor body* is destroyed at death;[3] and he says it in an incidental sort of way, as though that was something everybody knew. It seems reasonable that there should be some continuity, how-ever tenuous, between this mortal body and the resur-rection one; but we shall have to wait for our own death to find out all about it. In the meantime, what of that risen body, that final 'house' that each man's spirit will receive at the Last Day?

[1] Phil. 1.21-23.   [2] I Thess. 4.14.
[3] St Augustine, *De Doctrina Christiana*, I.21.

It is with reference to that body that St Paul uses both the figure of the seed, and the expression that we know as 'this vile body' (Phil. 3.20 f.). 'Vile' is a word that has changed its meaning since the Authorized Version was made in the seventeenth century. Now it carries a suggestion of depravity and viciousness; then, like Latin *vilis*, it meant rather 'cheap' or 'not worth much' —inferior, but not positively bad. Actually, however, St Paul here uses not an adjective, but an adjectival phrase, which may be rendered 'this body *of our low estate*'.[1] This, he tells us, our Lord will change at his Return, making it like 'the body of his glory'—that is, the body he himself assumed at his resurrection, and in which he now lives. It is to illustrate and emphasize this staggering truth that—no doubt remembering our dear Lord's own words about the 'corn of wheat'—he uses in I Cor. 15 the figure of the seed, out of which by the grave and gate of death comes so amazingly the green and growing corn.

Putting all this together, we can see how right St Francis of Assisi was to call his body 'Brother Ass'. A man's body is the Siamese twin brother of his spirit now, and is to be for all eternity. In his present larval and imperfect state, however, his body is inferior to his spirit; its life is on a lower plane, and tension between it and spirit is inevitable. In consequence, the good of both—that is, of the whole man—requires that the relation between the brothers should be like that of an owner-master and his riding-beast.

[1] RV, 'The body of our humiliation'.

'This Vile Body'

The Christian whose life is based on sound theology about his body will both love and reverence it alike as brother and as ass. He will have a constant eye both to its present well-being and to the eternal future for which the present is preparing it. That does not mean that he will pamper it—far from it, for that would not be for its good, or for the spirit's. It means that he will treat it reasonably; he will make it do its work and serve his purpose and, to enable it to do so, he will give it food and rest sufficient for its needs. Some of us need to take serious stock of our conduct in this respect. While there are some who give in to their bodies overmuch, there are perhaps as many more who are so utterly obsessed with work that they flog their bodies, refuse to go to bed when they are ill, never have time to give their thoughts to others, reject all offers of help, have no hobbies, play no games, and never take a holiday. They may think they are being very noble, but really they are only being proud. Most of us have to get rather more work out of our bodies than those bodies are really good for. Many of us are nearly always tired, and some of us have been so nearly all our lives. All this, with all that it entails of sufferings small and great, is— as we have seen—part of the very substance of our 'living sacrifice', and of the means by which Christ's power is to be perfected. As such, it must all be *accepted* with both hands, but to accept is not to acquiesce. If your tiredness *can* be mitigated and your limitations lessened by legitimate means, then those means should be used. Brother Ass deserves his nosebag, and his sleep, and even his days off and quiet hours in which to browse in peace.

Another thing that Brother Ass deserves is grooming; his personal appearance is his master's responsibility and business. We, who are nourished by the sacraments, ourselves are constituted on the sacramental principle. The world of each of us is made up largely of the exteriors of other people, while our own exterior forms part of other people's worlds, rather than of our own. From this it follows that it is a great responsibility to have an exterior that other people must inevitably see, especially a face. Your face is really something that you make yourself. A baby starts with just the raw materials of a face, no more. But very soon its character begins to form its face, for better or for worse. There is a legend that, when Jesus was a boy and anyone in Nazareth was in distress, they used to say, 'Let us go and look upon the face of Mary's son'. Small wonder, for Love's self looked out of it. And love, and joy, and peace, and all the fruits of the Spirit[1] should look in the same way from every Christian face; so that even those who do not know what they are seeing may be helped towards God, nonetheless, and warmed beside his fire. This does in fact happen quite a lot. St Athanasius had a face that was a constant blessing to his friends. Of our own Bishop King of Lincoln someone said, 'This is the face a man would have if he were really himself. This is the face that Love would normally wear.' The twelfth-century mystic, William of St Thierry, saw in this

[1] Gal. 5.22 f.

phenomenon—which we have all of us encountered more or less[1]—the actual beginning of the resurrection.[2]

Of course you do not have to think what you are looking like; that would defeat your object, for it would mean your inward eye was turned upon yourself, and not on God. But you do need to bear in mind that your face—yes, and your clothes and your whole bearing too—reflect the way you feel and think, and that other people willynilly must benefit or suffer from the net result. To be as easy on the eye—and ear—as possible is part of every Christian's debt of charity towards his neighbour.

[1] We all know the truth of Prov. 17.22. 'A merry heart doeth good like a medicine, but a broken spirit drieth up the bones', and both are expressed in the face.

[2] *The Meditations of William of St. Thierry*, tr. CSMV, Mowbrays, 1954, p. 95.

15

CONCLUSION

IN THIS BOOK we have frequently quoted St Paul, whose ceaseless labours, journeys, and afflictions surely entitle him to be considered as the busy Christian's patron saint. In conclusion we will quote another saint, who himself quotes St Paul, and who, although he was a monk, led a life so strenuous and full that, if two patrons are permissible, he certainly might fill the second place —Saint Bernard of Clairvaux: [1]

'For you, my brethren, who are already on the road to the heavenly kingdom, my sole anxiety is lest you should be daunted by the thought of prolonged life here on earth, and doubt if you can bear its load of suffering day after day. But you must remember that, as the apostle says, "The sufferings of this present time are not worthy to be compared with the glory that shall be revealed in us." [2] That is a lovely and inclusive promise. We are not going merely to stand by as gaping lookers-on; the glory is to be revealed not outside us, but *in* us.

[1] The quotation that follows is from St Bernard, *Sermones de Diversis*, I, 4, 6-8. The translation is that which I appended to *The Threefold Gift of Christ*, by Brother Bernard a thirteenth or fourteenth-century namesake of the saint), Mowbrays, 1954.　　　　　　　　　　　　　　　[2] Rom. 8.18.

For we shall see God face to face, not as external to us, but as in us, and as All in all. When he fills the whole earth with his glory, how much more will he fill the soul! "We shall be filled with the good things of thy house,"[1] the psalmist says. And why do I say that the glory will be seen not only by but in us? Because it is in us now, already; but then it will be revealed. For "*now* we are the sons of God; but it doth not yet appear what we shall be."[2]

'In this life, scarcely any of God's gifts serve us at will. Some things appear to serve us, but they do so only at the cost of our own toil, and after we have first served them. Beasts of burden, for instance, give us no help unless we first rear and tame and care for them. The earth itself, which should be more our own, does not supply our needs without the sweat of our brow; and even when we cultivate it, it gives us thorns and thistles. And all the other things, if you come to think about it, require from us far more service than they give; not to mention the things that are ready to do us active harm, like fire that burns, water that drowns, and wild beasts that slay. That is the way things are; but all the same the apostle is not lying when he says that "all things work together for good for them that love God, to them that are the called according to his purpose".[3] You notice that he says they "work together" for our good, not that they serve our wishes. They serve our profit and salvation, not our desire and

[1] Ps. 64.5 (Latin); cf. 65.4 (English).　　[2] See I John 3.2.
[3] Rom. 8.28.

will. And these things include even such no-things as vexation and sickness and death—yes, and sin too, for do not even a man's sins work together for his good when they make him humbler and more fervent and more careful of his steps?

'All these things, therefore, are the first fruits of the Spirit and of the Kingdom, the foretaste of glory, the beginning of power, and as it were the pledge of the inheritance that our Father is going to give us. But "when that which is perfect is come, then that which is in part will be done away",[1] and all things will be ordered after our desire; for profit and pleasure will then be made inseparably one. And that, assuredly, will be the eternal weight of glory of which the apostle says, "Our light affliction, which is but for a moment, worketh for us a far more exceeding and eternal weight of glory."[2]

'Go along with you, then, you grumbler who says, "It is too long, too difficult, I cannot carry such huge burdens every day!" The apostle calls his burden light and passing; and you have certainly not had five scourgings from the Jews of forty stripes save one, as he had; nor have you spent a day and a night in the depths of the sea! *You* have not laboured more than all,[3] nor—lastly—have you yet resisted unto blood![4] The sufferings of the present are not worthy to be compared with the future glory, because the tribulation is light and passing, and the glory is eternal, and an exceeding

[1] I Cor. 13.10.   [2] II Cor. 4.17.   [3] II Cor. 11.23-28.
[4] See Heb. 12.4.

weight. Why, then, do you worry about how long you may have to live? The time is passing, and the suffering with it; but with the glory that rewards the labour it is otherwise. That has no change, no end; it abides for ever, entire and the same. We drink our suffering drop by drop, successively in time; but the reward of glory is a river, a flooding river that never flows away.

'The apostle speaks of the eternal weight of glory. What we are promised is not a glorious garment, or a glorious house, but *glory*, glory itself. The hope of the righteous is gladness, not merely something glad. Men rejoice in food, and pleasures, and riches, and even in vice; but joys like that burn themselves out like a candle, and there is weeping at the end of them. But what God has laid up for us is purest, liquid honey, not honey in the comb; the treasure that he has in store for us is joy and life and glory, pleasure and happiness and gaiety and exultation, in themselves; and all these things are gathered into one, even as Jerusalem is compacted together into one.[1]

'And what is this oneness, save that which the apostle describes by saying that "God shall be All in all"?[2] This is our reward, our crown, our prize; and God grant us so to run towards it that we may obtain it! A sensible farmer who wants a plentiful harvest never thinks the sowing-time too long, my brethren. And your days are numbered, no less than the hair of your head, and no moment of your days shall perish either. Having then such a promise, most beloved, let us not fail nor

---

[1] Ps. 121.3 (Latin); cf. 122.3 (English).   [2] I Cor. 15.28.

This is Life

be weary, neither let us complain that the burden of
Christ is heavy, for we have his own word for it that it
is light, and his yoke easy too;[1] but rather, in face of
every load that we carry today, let us consider the
eternal weight of glory . . .'

Here and hereafter, 'This is life' indeed!

[1] Matt. 11.29 f.

INDEX OF BIBLICAL REFERENCES

Index of Biblical References